Toddlers

BIG BOOK
of Coloring
Pages & Activities

BIG BOOK OF COLORING PAGES AND ACTIVITIES FOR TODDLERS
Published by David C Cook
4050 Lee Vance Drive
Colorado Springs, CO 80918 U.S.A.

Integrity Music Limited, a Division of David C Cook
Brighton, East Sussex BN1 2RE, England

The graphic circle C logo is a registered trademark of David C Cook.

All rights reserved. Permission is granted to reproduce all pages in this book for ministry purposes only—not for resale.

All Scripture quotations are taken from the Holy Bible, NEW INTERNATIONAL VERSION®, NIV®. Copyright © 1973, 2011 by Biblica, Inc.® Used by permission. All rights reserved worldwide. NEW INTERNATIONAL VERSION® and NIV® are registered trademarks of Biblica, Inc. Use of either trademark for the offering of goods or services requires the prior written consent of Biblica, Inc.

ISBN 978-0-8307-7237-7

© 2018 David C Cook

The content included in this book was originally published in *God Loves Me Coloring Pages (Ages 1–2)* by Standard Publishing in 2006 © Standard Publishing, ISBN 978-0-7847-1796-7.

Cover Design: James Hershberger
Illustrator: Mary Bausman

Printed in the United States of America
3 4 5 6 7 8 9 10 11 12

080422

Contents

Introduction 6

God Made Me
God Made Me. 7
God Made Me Activities 8
God made my eyes. 10
Thank You, God, for my eyes. 11
God made my ears. 12
Thank You, God, for my ears. 13
God made my nose. 14
My nose can smell flowers. 15
Thank You, God, for my nose. 16
God made my mouth. 17
Thank You, God, for my mouth. 18
God made my arms. .19
Thank You, God, for my arms. 20
God made my hands. 21
Thank You, God, for my hands. 22
God made my legs. 23
Thank You, God, for my legs. 24
God made my legs. Thank You, God! 25
God made my feet. 26
Thank You, God, for my feet. 27
I'm glad God made my feet. 28
God made all of me. .29
Thank You, God, for making me. 30
God made me! Thank You, God! 31

God Made People
God Made People. 32
God Made People Activities. 33
God made baby girls. 35
God made baby boys. 36
God made babies. 37

God made big girls. 38
God made big boys. .39
God made little children and bigger children. 40
God made mothers. .41
God made fathers. 42
God made grandmas. 43
God made grandpas. .44
God made brothers. .45
God made sisters. 46
God made leaders. 47
God made teachers. .48
God made doctors. 49
God made firefighters. 50
God made police officers. 51

God Made Food
God Made Food 52
God Made Food Activities 53
God made vegetables. 55
God made vegetables. 56
Thank You, God, for vegetables. 57
God made fruit. 58
Thank You, God, for fruit. 59
God made bread. 60
God made cereal. 61
God made water. 62
God made juice. 63

God Made the World
God Made the World. 64
God Made the World Activities 65
God made the sky. 67
God made clouds. 68
God made water and land. Thank You, God! 69

God made birds. 70
God made birds that fly. .71
God made birds that walk. 72
God made big birds. 73
God made little birds. 74
God made the sun. 75
God made the moon. 76
God made the stars. 77
God made the ocean. 78
God made puddles. 79
God made mountains. 80
God made dirt. 81
God made fish. 82
God made little fish. 83
God made big fish. 84
God made trees. 85
God made plants. 86
God made bushes. 87
God made flowers. 88
God made bugs with legs. 89
God made bugs that fly. 90
God made puppies. 91
God made kittens. 92
God made elephants. 93
God made giraffes. 94
God made horses. 95
God made cows. 96
God made animals with hard shells. 97
God made animals with soft fur. 98
God made animals that crawl. 99
God made animals that jump. 100
God made fall. 101
God made winter. 102
God made spring. 103
God made summer. 104
God made everything. Thank You, God! 105

God Gives Me Good Things

God Gives Me Good Things 106
God Gives Me Good Things Activities 107
God gives me food. 109
Thank You, God, for food. 110
God gives me apples to eat. 111
God gives me clothes. .112
Thank You, God, for clothes. 113
God gives me shoes. 114
My clothes keep me warm. 115
God gives me a place to live. 116
God gives me a place to sleep. 117
God gives me good things. 118
Thank You, God, for good things. 119
God gives me water. 120
God gives me water. 121
Thank You, God, for good water. 122

God Cares for Me

God Cares for Me 123
God Cares for Me Activities 124
God cares for me in the morning. 126
God cares for me when I am waking up. 127
God cares for me when I am eating. 128
God cares for me when I am thirsty. 129
God cares for me when I am playing. 130
God cares for me when I am playing. 131
God cares for me when I go to new places. 132
God cares for me at night. 133
God cares for me when I am sleeping. 134

Jesus Loves Me

Jesus Loves Me 135
Jesus Loves Me Activities 136
Jesus loves everyone. .138
Jesus loves mothers. 139
Jesus loves fathers. 140

Jesus loves families... 141
Jesus loves families... 142
I love my family... 143
Jesus loves children... 144
Jesus loves children... 145
Jesus loves children... 146
Jesus loves children... 147
Jesus loves you too!... 148
Jesus loves people... 149
Jesus loves people... 150
Jesus loves people... 151
Jesus loves people... 152
Jesus loves people... 153
Jesus loves you... 154
Jesus loves me... 155

My Church
I Go to Church ... 156
I Go to Church Activities ... 157
I learn about Jesus at church. I am happy
  at church!... 159
I sing at church... 160
I sing about Jesus... 161
I can pray at church. I am happy at church!... 162
I pray at church... 163
God hears me pray... 164
I learn at church... 165
I learn from my teacher... 166
I learn God loves me... 167
I learn about Jesus... 168
I have friends at church... 169
I am a friend to others... 170
God gives me friends... 171

Noah
God Makes a Promise... 172
Noah Activities... 173

Noah was a good man... 175
God told Noah to build a big boat... 176
Noah worked hard... 177
Noah obeyed God... 178
Noah loved God and built a big boat... 179
Noah brought animals into the ark... 180
Noah brought two of every animal... 181
Noah brought tall animals... 182
Noah brought big animals... 183
Noah brought small animals... 184
The animals got into the boat... 185
God sent rain... 186
There was a flood... 187
The ark floated on the water... 188
The rain stopped... 189
God put a rainbow in the sky... 190

Baby Jesus
Baby Jesus Was Born... 191
Baby Jesus Activities ... 192
Joseph and Mary were married... 195
Mary was Jesus' mother... 196
Jesus was born... 197
Baby Jesus was born... 198
Jesus is God's Son... 199
Joseph and Mary loved Jesus... 200
Angels sang the night Jesus was born... 201
Shepherds came to visit Jesus... 202
The shepherds visited Jesus... 203
The shepherds were happy Jesus was born... 204
Wise men saw a star... 205
The star led the wise men to Jesus... 206
The wise men gave Jesus gifts... 207

HeartShaper® Toddlers & 2s
  Scope and Sequence ... 208

Introduction

Big Book of Coloring Pages and Activities for Toddlers is designed to offer options for teachers of one and two year olds. With over 160 coloring and texture pages, more than 50 teaching ideas, plus a special holiday section, this book is a must-have resource for every classroom! Keep reading to find out how to use each element in this book to make the most of everything offered here.

Coloring Pages
Toddlers are exploring and learning about their environment moment by moment. Some children will be learning to use crayons for the first time. Most children will scribble-color these pages. The simple statements at the bottom of each page explain the picture and will help you talk to the toddlers about God, His Word, and their world.

Texture Pages
These pages are offered to help you do something more with the toddlers These simple variations on coloring pages make them more engaging and are designed to be appropriate for the skill level of toddlers.

Activity Pages
Each category in this coloring book includes activity ideas to reinforce the topic. These are simple ideas that you can do with the children in your class to help them explore and connect with the Bible truth you're teaching. Some activities will require some preparation before class, so please read them in advance to make sure you have everything you need to use them in class.

Make the most of every opportunity with toddlers. Explore and create with them as you help them discover God's love!

God Made Me

Supplies: Washable ink pads

Instructions: Gather the children and explain that God made each of them in a special way. We are all different from each other. Just like our fingerprints, no two of us are exactly the same. Have the children look at their fingers and tell them that fingertips make fingerprints. With the children sitting at the table, let them put their fingers on the washable ink pads and stamp their fingerprints on the pictures of the hands. Remind the children that God made them. Be sure to wash the ink off their hands.

God Made Me Activities

Popcorn Ball

Supplies
- Small, lightweight blanket or beach towel
- Inflatable ball

Gather children and ask everyone to hold onto part of the edge of the blanket or towel. Try to space the children evenly around the outside edge. An adult should be on either side of the blanket. Throw the ball onto the middle of the blanket and tell children to use their arms and hands God made to move the blanket up and down. Say "Up" and "Down" to help them coordinate their movements. The ball should bounce around like a piece of popcorn.

Testing Textures

Supplies
- 5' length of paper
- Several different-textured materials, including: fine sandpaper, felt, vinyl, fur, velvet, crumpled foil or wrapping paper
- Several cotton balls
- Tacky glue

Before class, use glue to attach the textured material and cotton balls to the paper. Use large enough pieces for the children to be able to really experience the textures of the items. Add other textured items if desired. When the glue is dry, gently roll up the paper to transport to class. In class, ask children to crawl over the paper, using their hands and knees God made to feel all the different textures. Ask them about each texture. Is it rough? Is it smooth? As an alternative, children can remove their shoes and socks and walk over the paper with their bare feet. This will allow them to feel with their feet all the different textures God made.

God Made Me Banner

Supplies
- Large length of white paper
- Markers
- Construction paper in various colors
- Scissors
- Glue
- Crayons
- Pushpins or reusable adhesive

Before class, draw several large stick figures on the paper—about 2' apart—one for each child in your class. Using construction paper, cut out several dresses, pants, and shirts to fit the figures. Write in big letters above the figures "God Made Me!" In class, allow each child to choose a figure that will represent himself or herself. Write children's names underneath the stick figures. Help them pick out some clothes for their figures and glue them on. While some children are gluing on clothes, others can be using crayons to color their hair and facial features. Younger toddlers may just scribble. While working, talk about how God made all children so different and so wonderful. Make sure everyone finishes all of the figures. Display the banner in class or hallway for the rest of the unit.

Senses Table

Supplies
- Cotton balls saturated with scents like vanilla extract, perfume, lemon juice, and peppermint extract
- Small bags
- Small musical instruments
- Brightly colored blocks or balls
- Bananas
- Apples
- Grapes
- Knife
- Small plates
- Electronic device *(optional)*

Before class, place saturated cotton balls in separate bags and cut fruit into bite-size pieces. Instead of musical instruments, you could record several different sounds (like dog barking, doorbell, telephone, birds chirping) on an electronic device. Tell the children they are going to use the eyes, ears, nose, and mouth God made. Hold a bag open for the children to smell. Tell them to use the noses God made to smell. Let them smell the scent. Next, let the children play the instruments or listen to the recorded sounds. Remind them that God made our ears to hear. Hold up the blocks or balls and ask them to use their eyes to tell you the colors. They will also use their mouths God made to taste the fruits you cut into bite-size pieces.

God made my eyes.

Thank You, God, for my eyes.

God made my ears.

Thank You, God, for my ears.

God made my nose.

My nose can smell flowers.

Thank You, God, for my nose.

God made my mouth.

Thank You, God, for my mouth.

God made my arms.

Thank You, God, for my arms.

God made my hands.

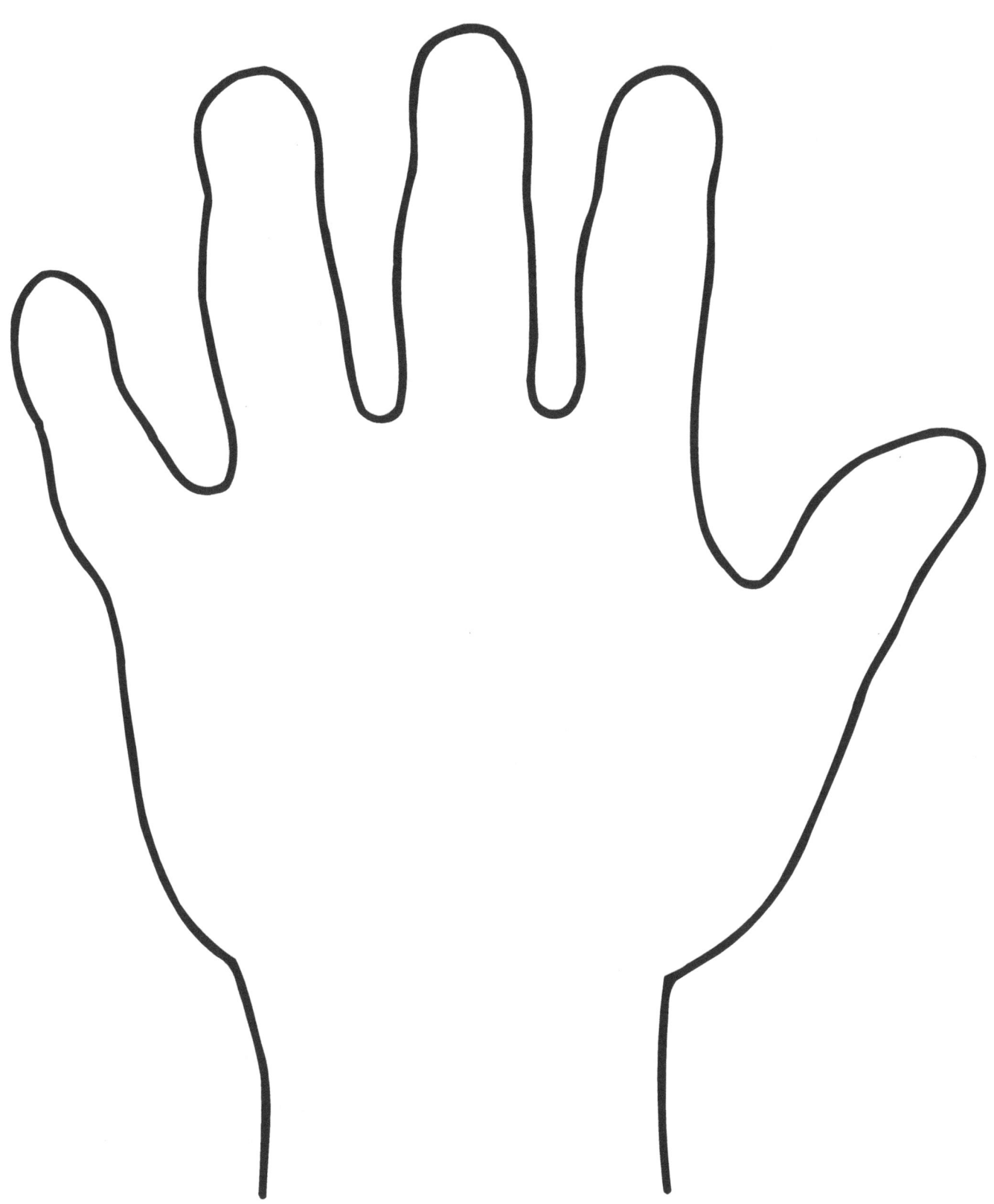

Thank You, God, for my hands.

God made my legs.

Thank You, God, for my legs.

God made my legs. Thank You, God!

God made my feet.

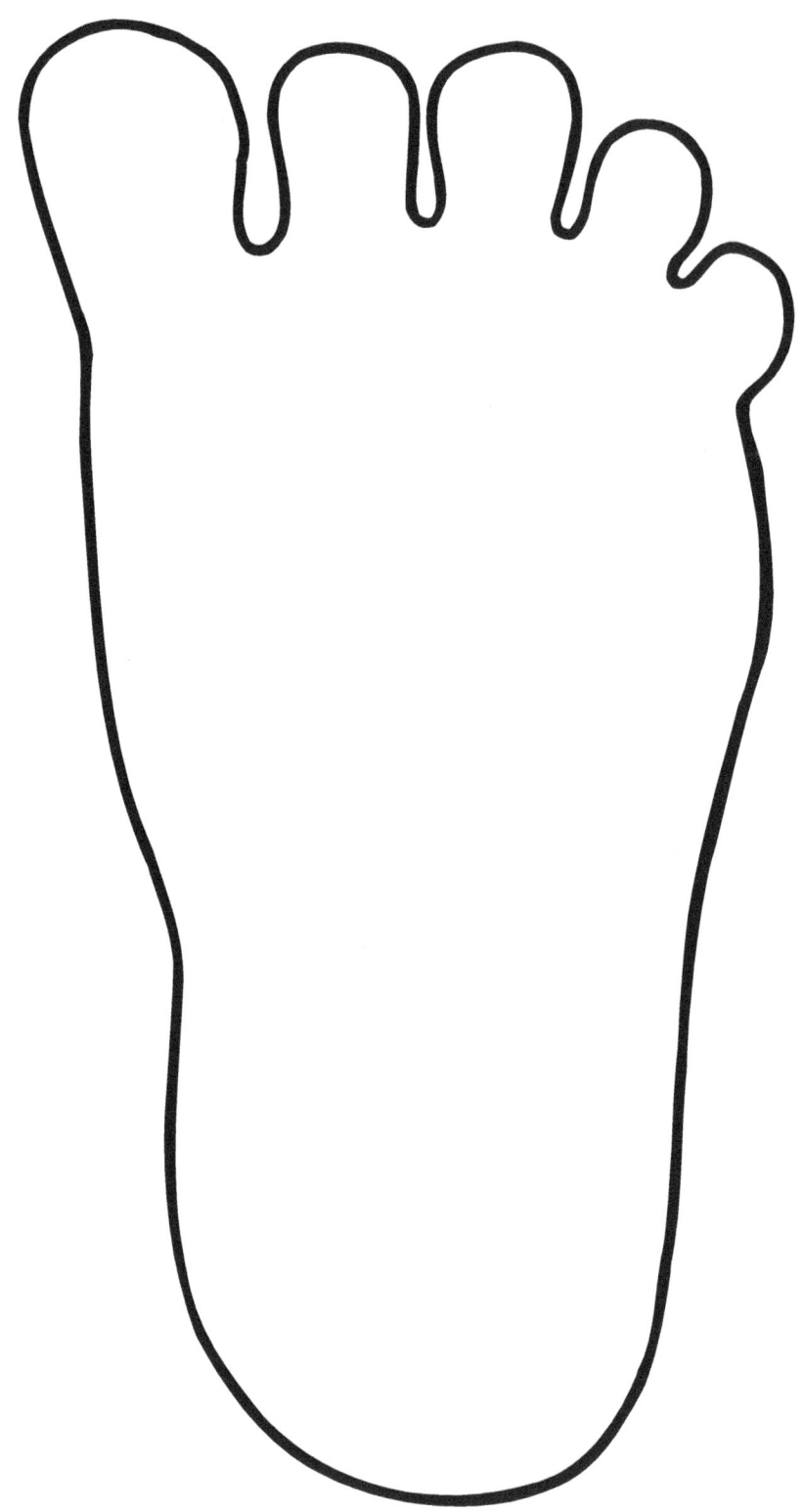

Thank You, God, for my feet.

I'm glad God made my feet.

God made all of me.

Thank You, God, for making me.

God made me! Thank You, God!

God Made People

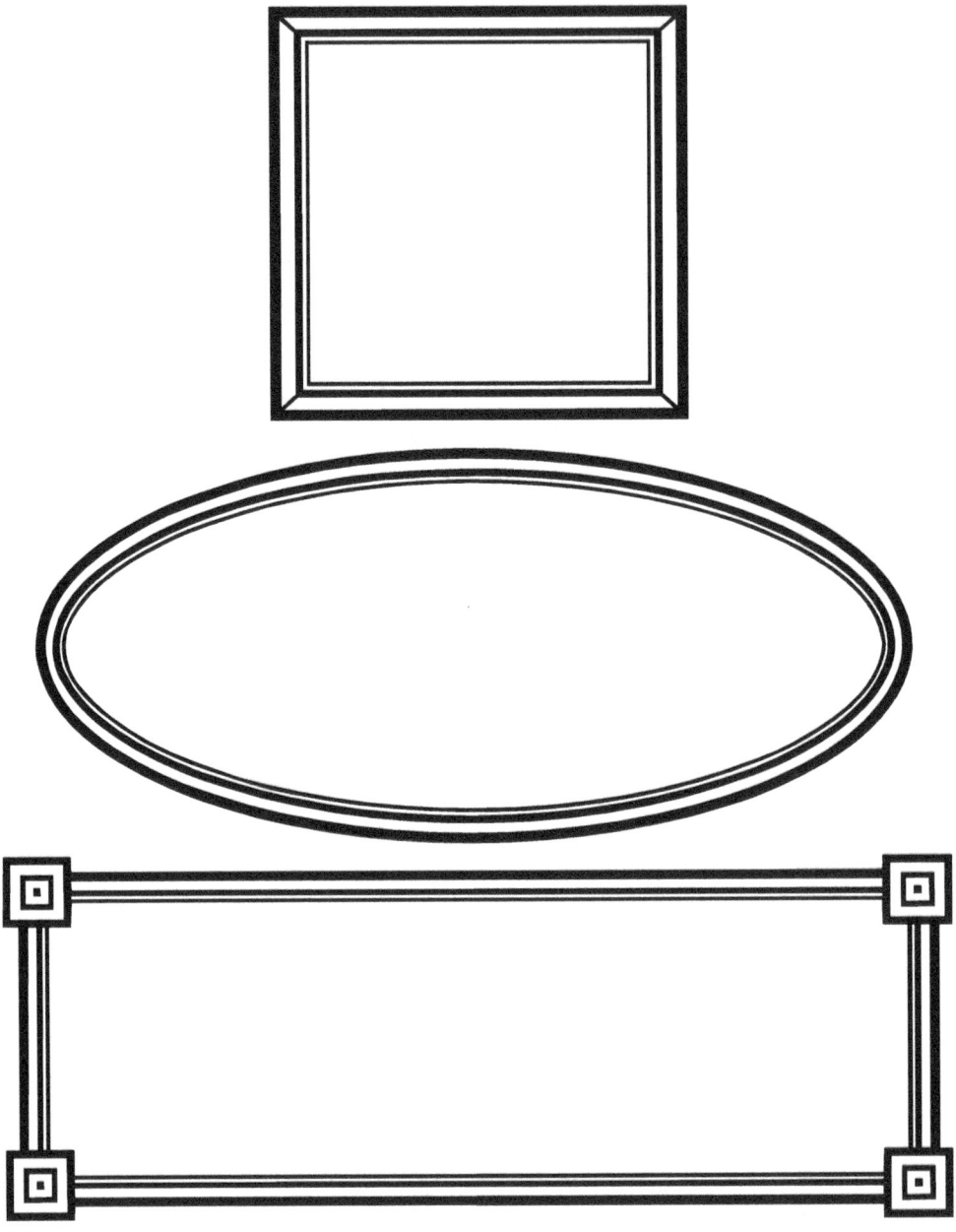

Supplies: Magazines, scissors, glue sticks

Instructions: Before class, cut out magazine pictures of different types of people. Be sure both males and females are represented. Mix up your picture selection so some people are working, some are with children, some are cooking, etc. During class, have the children choose different pictures of people and glue them onto their picture frames. Explain to them that God made all people.

God Made People Activities

People Puppets

Supplies
- Magazines
- Scissors
- Construction paper
- Glue stick
- Craft sticks

Before class, cut out pictures of several different types of people from magazines. Try to find men, women, children, babies, and different types of workers. Then glue the pictures to construction paper to make them sturdier. In class, allow children to select one or two of the people to make into puppets. Help children choose some people and use a glue stick to attach the people to the craft sticks. While working, talk about how God made different types of people and what types of people He made. After puppets are finished, encourage children to play with them. Make some puppets yourself, before class, and use your puppets to stage a show for the children.

Care Center

Supplies
- Baby dolls
- Doll clothes
- Toy baby bottle
- Child chairs
- Toy doctor accessories

Before class, set up part of the room as a Care Center, where children can pretend to care for others as parents, grandparents, firefighters, police officers, and doctors. Set up small chairs, tables, baby beds, and baby dolls. Tell the children they are going to the Care Center to practice caring for others. Show them how to hold the babies and feed them with the toy bottles. They can pretend to care for the babies as parents and grandparents do, changing and feeding the babies. Talk about how God made babies and children and how God made parents and grandparents to take care of babies and children! Other children can pretend to be doctors. Emphasize that God made doctors, firefighters, police officers, and families to help and care for each other.

Helper Town

Supplies
- Large carpet play mat with roads or masking tape to make roads on the floor
- Small preschool toy vehicles, including mail trucks, tow trucks, police cars, or fire trucks
- Preschool toy people to ride in the vehicles

Spread out the mat in the classroom. Encourage children to take a car and play along the outside of the mat. Ask the children to choose toy people to ride in their vehicles. As they play and drive their vehicles through the town, remind them what firefighters, police officers, etc., do in a town. They can pretend to be a firefighter driving to put out a fire. They could also be a police officer helping other cars to drive safely. Another car could be a family driving to the grocery store, the park, or to church. Remind them as they play that God made families to love and care for each other.

Follow the Leader

Supplies
- Several baby dolls
- Several children's books
- Several toy phones

Line up children and tell them to follow you around the room and do what you do. Tell them you are going to pretend to be all different kinds of people God made. First pretend to be a baby, crawling and making crying sounds. Encourage children to copy and follow you. Next tell them you are a big brother or sister, stretching up tall and walking as tall as you can. Continue your walk by pretending to be various people, like a soldier or a member of a marching band or a runner. At the end of your walk, sit down by the baby dolls, books, and toy phones. Tell children you are now pretending to be mommies, daddies, and grandparents—holding babies, talking on the phone, reading the newspaper, or reading books. Thank God for making our families to take care of us and for making all people.

God made baby girls.

God made baby boys.

God made babies.

God made big girls.

God made big boys.

God made little children and bigger children.

God made mothers.

God made fathers.

God made grandmas.

God made grandpas.

God made brothers.

God made sisters.

God made leaders.

God made teachers.

God made doctors.

God made firefighters.

God made police officers.

God Made Food

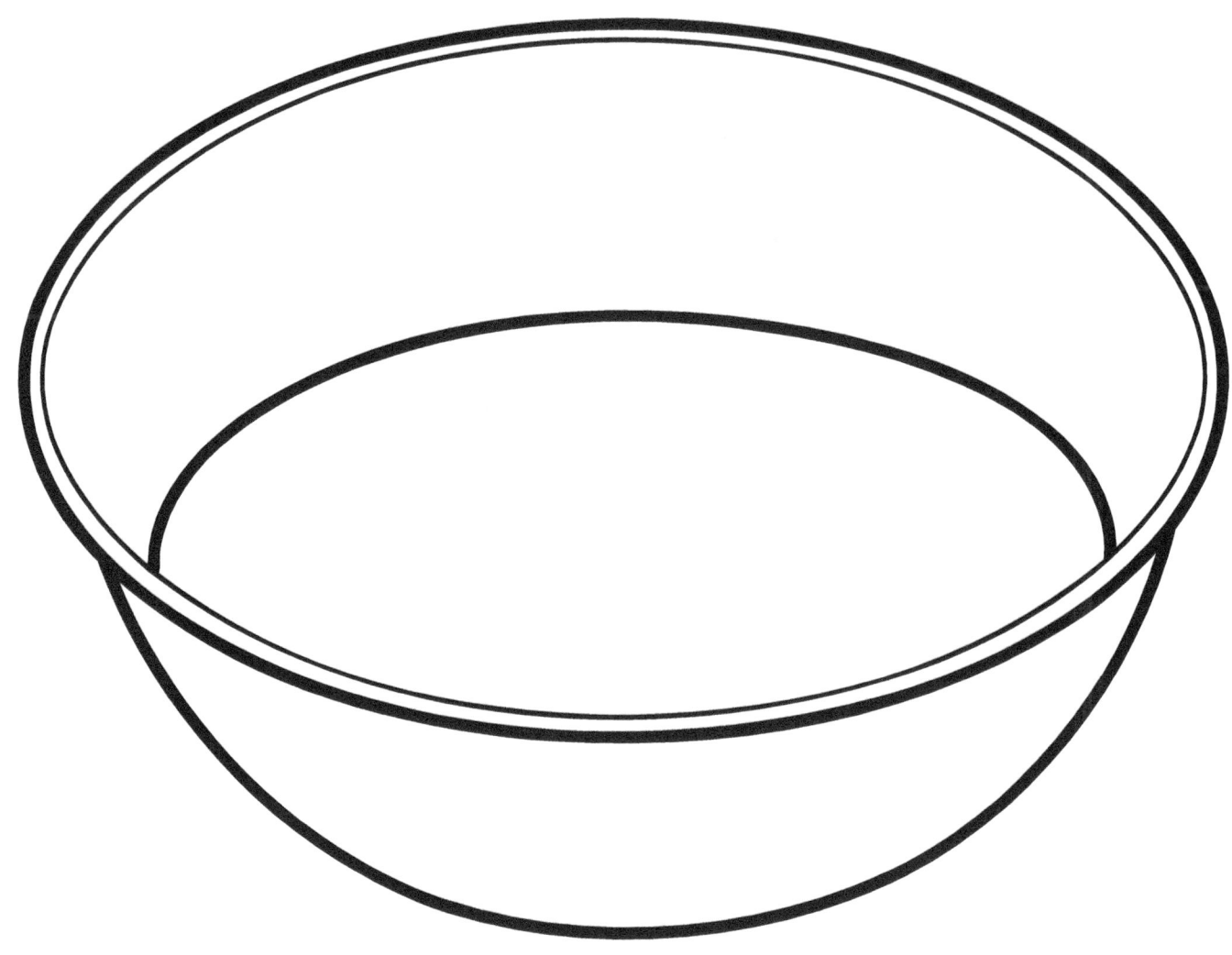

Supplies: Box of O-shaped cereal, bag of shredded carrots, paper plates, glue sticks

Instructions: Gather the children together and tell them they will be learning about all the good food God made for them to eat. At the table, pour O-shaped cereal and shredded carrots on paper plates for the children to share. Help the kids choose pieces of carrots and cereal to glue onto the picture of the bowl. Remind the children God made all good foods for them to eat and to help them grow up to be big and strong.

God Made Food Activities

Tasting Bags

Supplies
- Bite-size cereal, like O-shaped cereal or wheat puffs
- Mini marshmallows
- Cheddar fish crackers
- Small bowls
- Plastic spoons, 1 for each child
- Resealable sandwich bags, 1 for each child

Before starting the activity, pour two types of cereal, marshmallows, and cheddar crackers into separate small bowls. Set the bowls in the center of the table. When children are seated, give each of them a spoon and a sandwich bag. Allow them to choose spoonfuls of the different foods to put in their tasting bags. For younger toddlers, help them by holding open the bags and guiding the spoon into the bag. Seal the bags and tell children to shake them up. You can have them eat their tasting bag mix while they are seated or save them to eat later. While children are working on their bags, talk about how God made food to help us grow up healthy and strong.

Stringing Rings

Supplies
- Construction paper
- Scissors
- Hole punch
- Marker
- Yarn
- Tape
- Paper plates
- Stickers with pictures of food
- Colored O-shaped cereal

Before class, cut 3" circles out of colored paper, one per child. Write "God Made Food" on each of the circles. Punch a hole in each circle. Cut 2' lengths of yarn and wrap tape around one end for easier stringing. Then tie a knot around one piece of cereal at the end of each string of yarn. Give each of the children a colored circle and have him or her put a few food stickers on it. Write their names on the back of the circles. Then pour a small amount of cereal on paper plates and tell them to string cereal on the yarn for a necklace. Younger children will need more help with this. String the circle on the yarn along with the cereal. When children are finished, tie the string together like a necklace. Remind them how thankful we are to God that He made food for us.

Growing Food

Supplies
- Plastic toy gardening tools
- Plastic toy food
- Tub of play sand

Give children gardening tools and tell them they are going to help grow food. Show them how to dig in the sand and plant a seed (toy food). Cover it up with sand and tell children how God sends rain and sunshine to grow plants. Then give them the toy food to dig up (or harvest) from the ground. Let them do all these things while you are talking. Tell children to pretend to be the growing plant. They can squat down near the floor. First, the seed is inside the ground. Then God sends rain and sunshine, and the plant comes up from the ground and grows taller and taller. As you are talking, show children how they can stand up until they are a tall plant with arms spread high. Tell them that growing plants are one way that God gives us good food to eat.

Food Hunt

Supplies
- Toy food: apples, bananas, oranges, grapes, bread, pizza, juice bottles, hot dogs, and hamburgers
- Paper lunch bags

Before class, hide the toy food around the classroom. Hide enough so each child can find several pieces of food. Be sure to hide them in easily seen places, where toddlers can spot them. Gather children and tell them they are going on a food hunt. Give each child a bag and supervise the children as they look around the classroom for the food. Some children might need more help than others. You might need to tell others to sit down after they've quickly found a few items. When each child has found a few items, pull out the items one at a time and identify them. Talk about how God made all food and gives it to us so we can be healthy and strong.

God made vegetables.

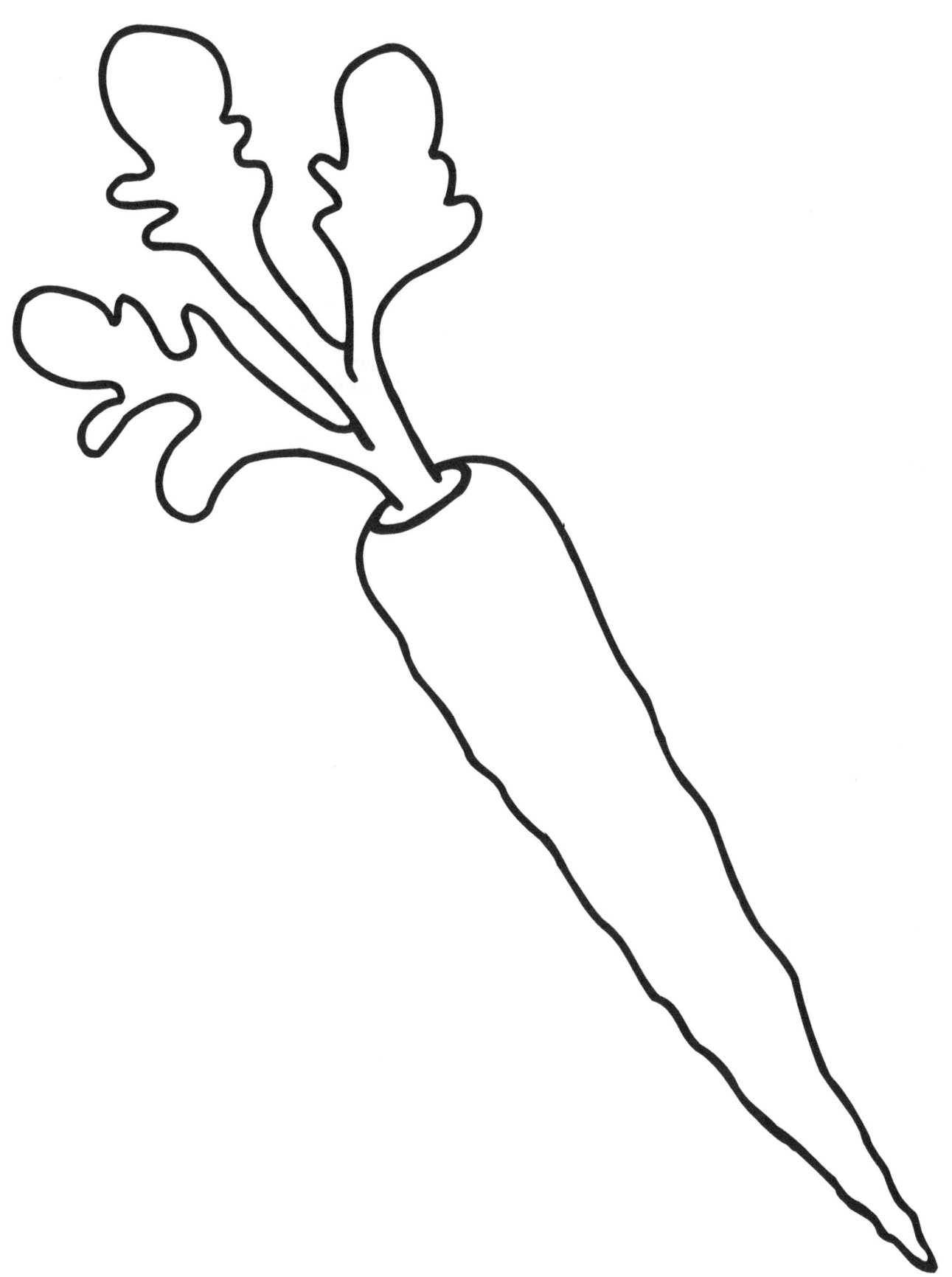

God made vegetables.

Thank You, God, for vegetables.

God made fruit.

Thank You, God, for fruit.

God made bread.

God made cereal.

God made water.

God made juice.

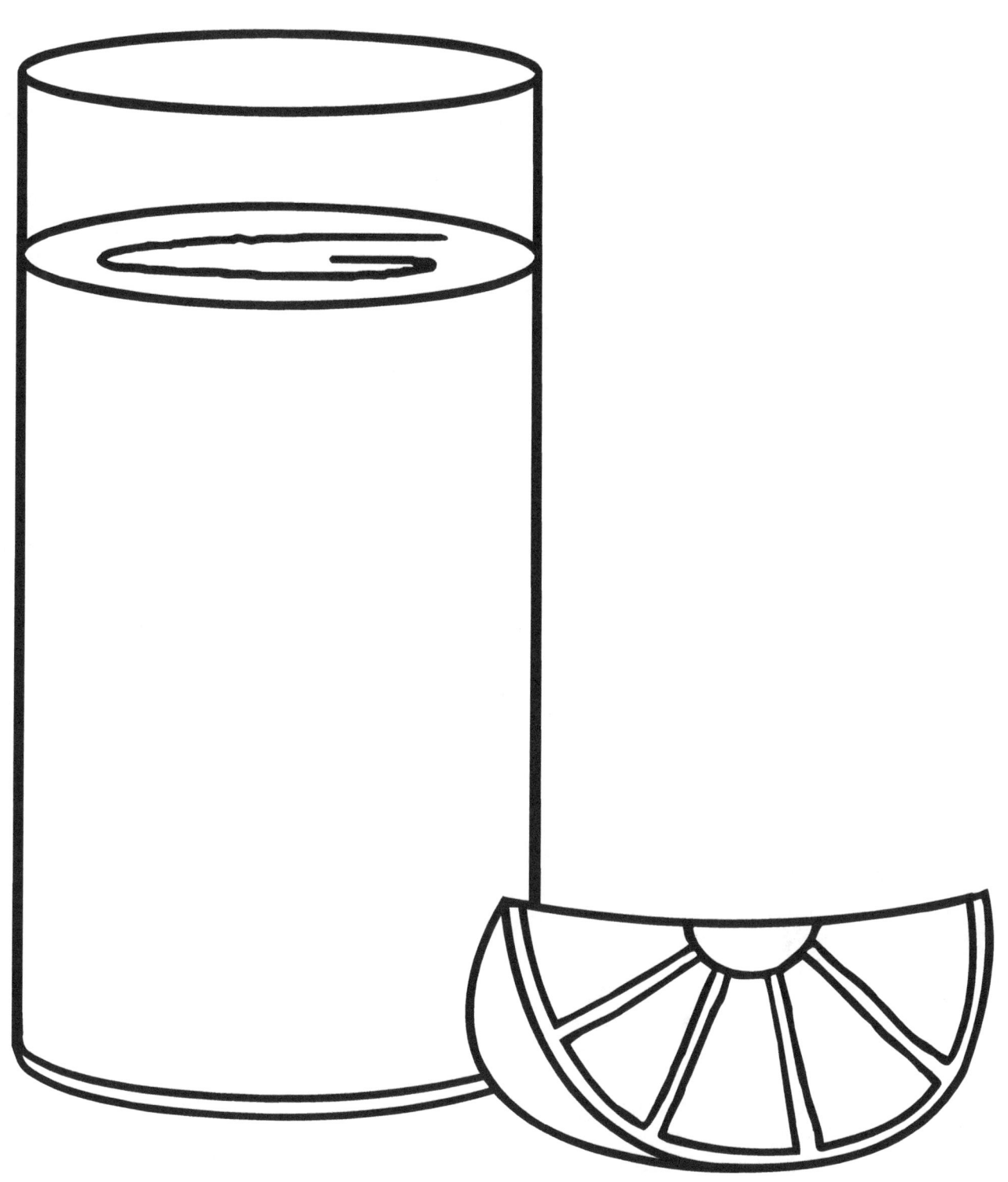

God Made the World

Supplies: Large crayons, stickers with flower designs (scratch 'n sniff, if possible).

Instructions: Have the children color the picture. Then peel off stickers and allow children to choose the ones they like to stick onto the coloring page. Explain to children that God made the world and all the things in it, like green grass and pretty flowers.

God Made the World

Pond Fishing

Supplies
- Colored construction paper
- Pen
- Scissors
- Adhesive magnet strip
- Empty paper towel rolls, 1 for each child
- Yarn
- Blue blanket or sheet

Before class, trace and cut out several fish shapes from colored paper. Cut a 1" piece from the magnet strip and affix to each fish. Tape 18" of yarn to the end of paper towel rolls to make fishing rods. On the other end of the yarn, tie a knot around a 2" piece of the magnet strip, with backing paper still on. Make sure that the magnetic side of the magnet is facedown. In class, spread a blue blanket on the floor and spread the fish on top, near the edges. Give children the "rods" and take them to the "pond" to go fishing. Have them stand around the outside of the blanket and try to "catch" the fish. Younger toddlers may need help guiding the magnets together. Talk about how God made ponds and lakes and the fish that live there.

Leaf Rubbings

Supplies
- Several medium-size leaves
- White paper
- Large crayons

Before class, scatter the leaves around the room or in an area where children can go on a leaf hunt. Take the children on a walk, allowing each to pick up a couple leaves. Talk about how God made trees and leaves that grow on them. If possible, you could also do this walk outside. At the table, give each child a sheet of paper. Show children how they can put the leaf under the paper and rub on it with a crayon. This will show the beautiful shape of the leaf God made. You will have to help some children by holding the paper or encouraging them to press a little harder. Let them do several rubbings until they have multiple leaves on their papers.

Water Play

Supplies
- Large plastic tub
- Water
- Small toy boats
- Small cups
- Live plants
- Large apples
- Sponges
- Towels
- Smocks *(optional)*

Fill a tub with 2" of water and set it on a towel. Put smocks on children *(optional)*. Tell them that when God made the world, He made water for us to drink and for plants and animals to drink too. He also made water so we could swim and wash our bodies and clothes. Allow children to play with boats and cups in the water tub. Help children, one at a time, get a small cup of water and water one of the plants that God made. You can help other children wash the apples God made. Be sure to supervise closely and have plenty of towels handy for this activity.

Reaching the Seasons

Supplies
- Marker
- Various colors of paper
- Scissors
- Yarn
- Tape

Before class, draw and cut out four different shapes to represent the four seasons, such as: orange or red leaf for fall; white snowflake for winter; light blue, purple, and green butterflies for spring; and yellow sun for summer. Attach each shape to a piece of yarn and tape it to the ceiling. Gather children under the shapes. Tell them you want them to find the shape for each season. When it's fall, the tree leaves turn pretty colors and fall down. Can you find the fall leaf? Talk about how God made fall and all the other seasons. When they find the leaf, ask them to "catch" it by reaching and jumping up. Do the same with all four seasons, asking them to find the seasonal shapes and then jump up to "catch" them.

God made the sky.

God made clouds.

God made water and land. Thank You, God!

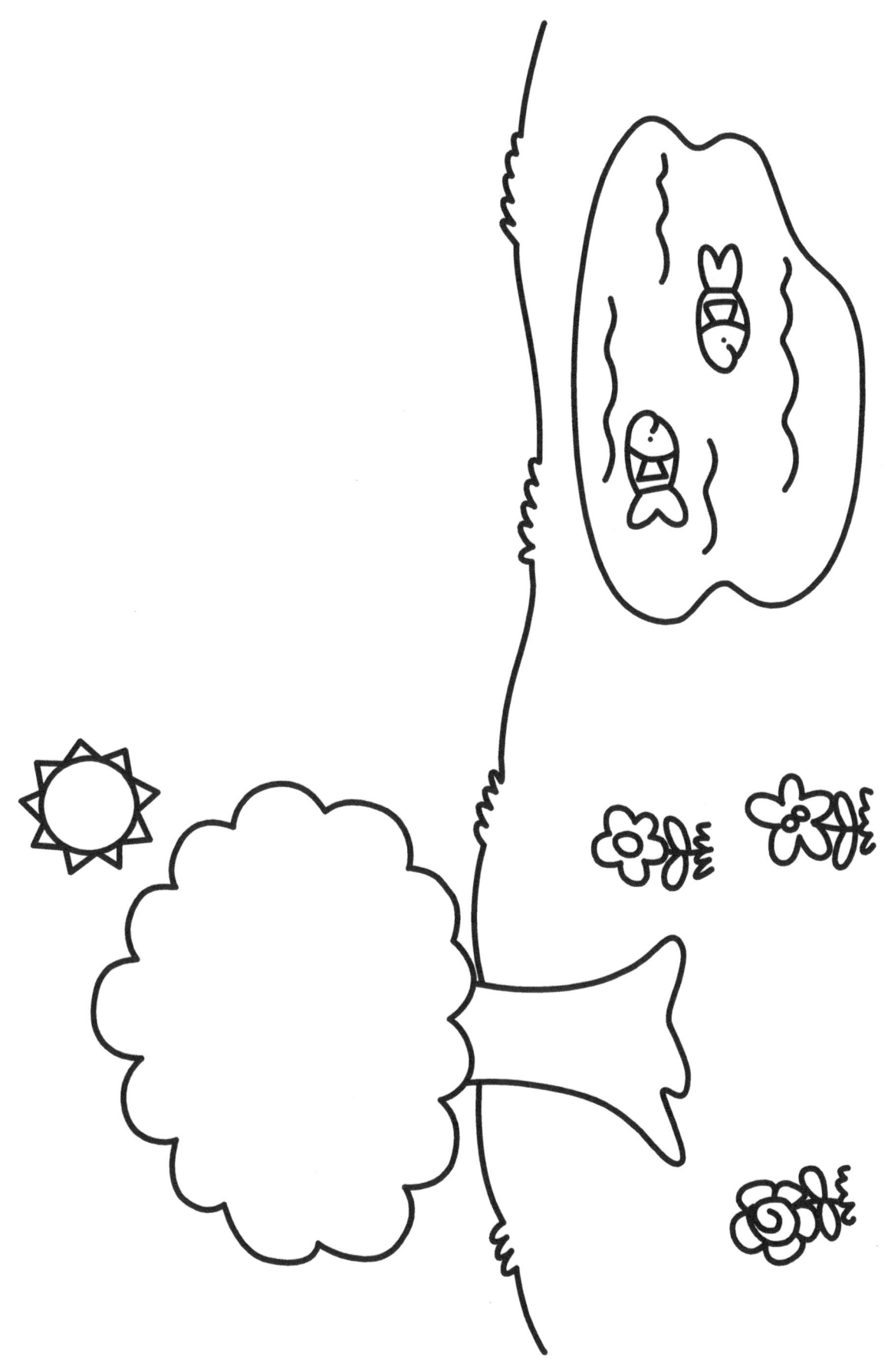

God made birds.

God made birds that fly.

God made birds that walk.

God made big birds.

God made little birds.

God made the sun.

God made the moon.

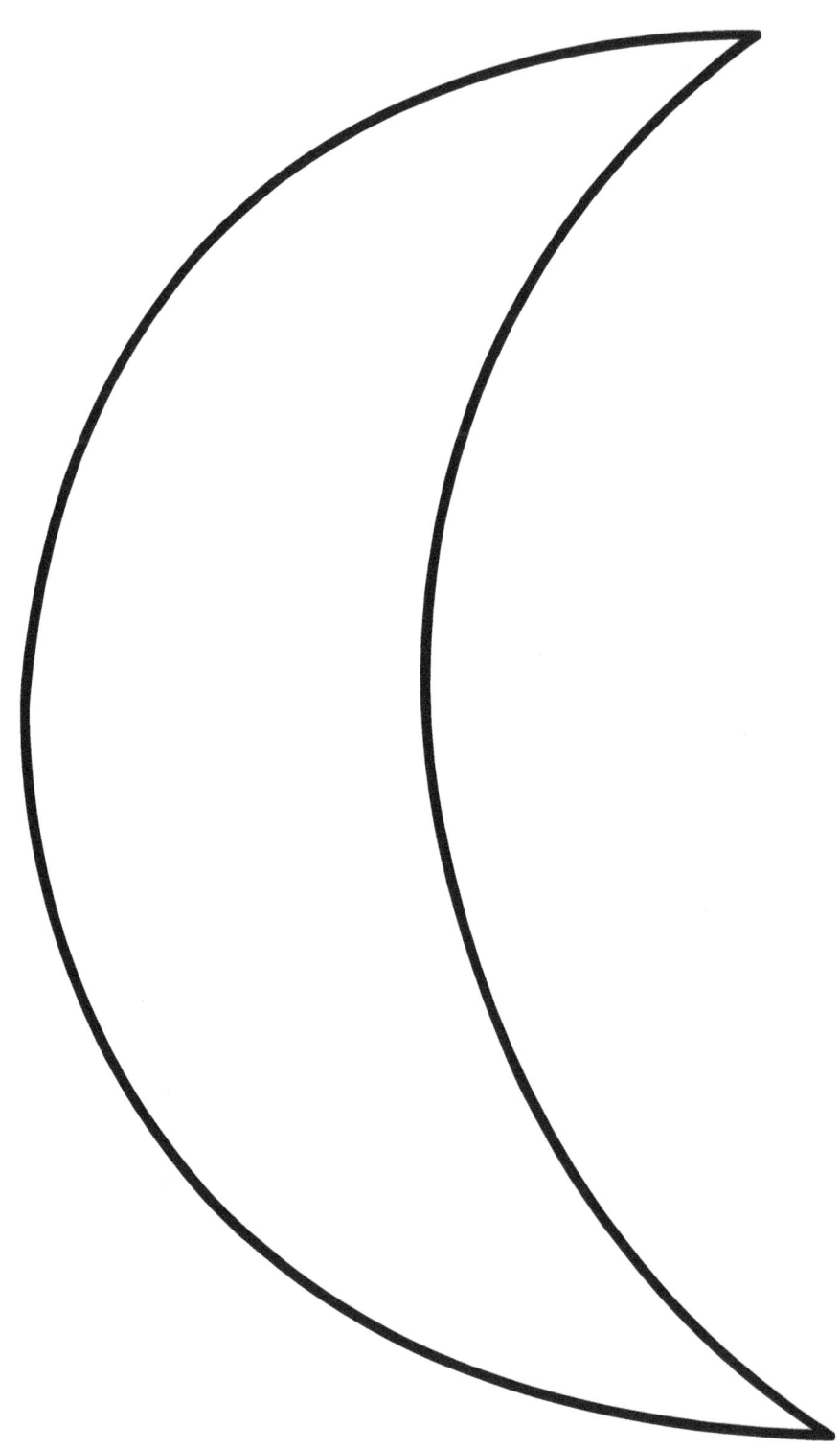

God made the stars.

God made the ocean.

God made puddles.

God made mountains.

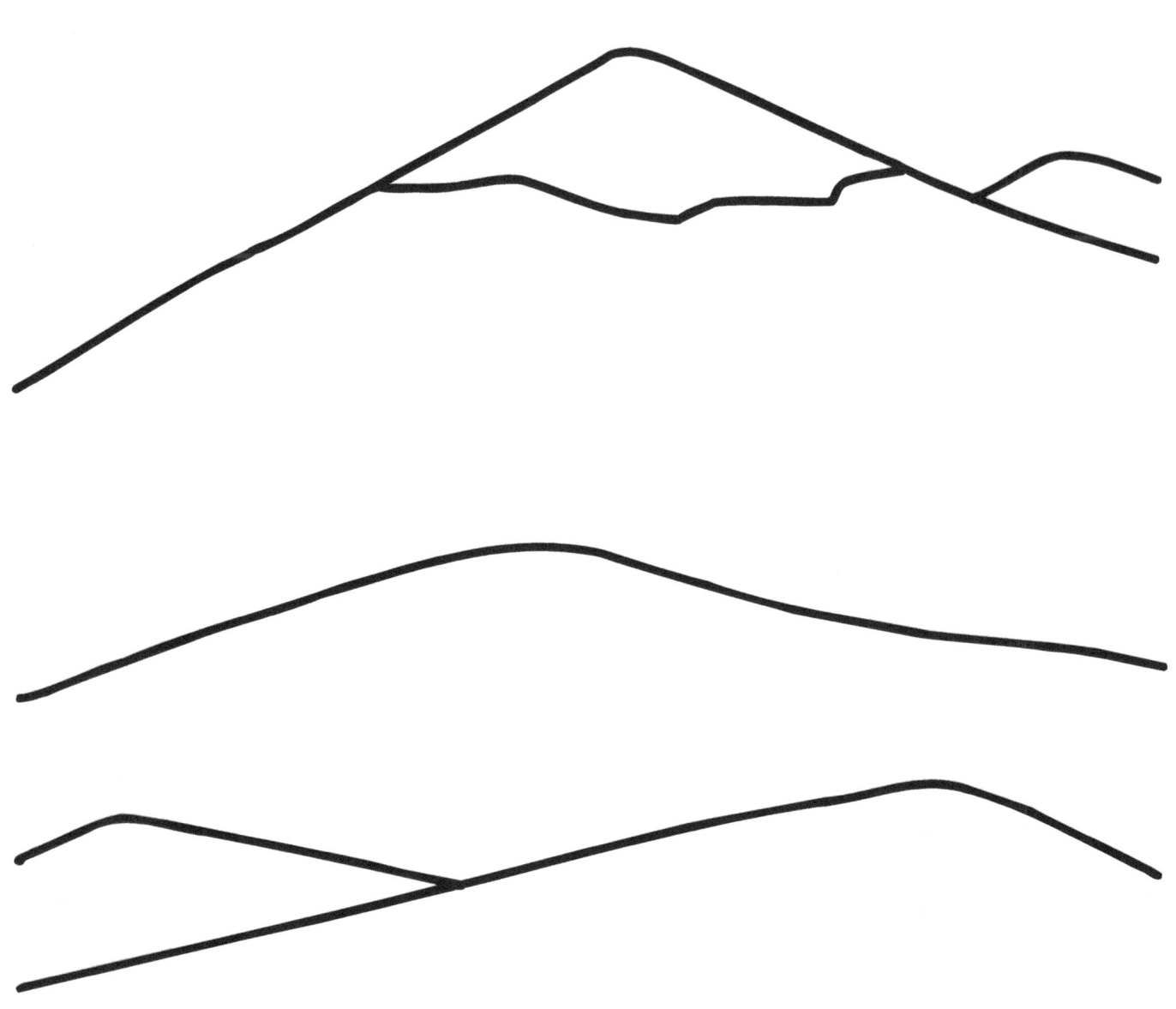

God made dirt.

God made fish.

God made little fish.

God made big fish.

God made trees.

God made plants.

God made bushes.

God made flowers.

God made bugs with legs.

Title God made bugs that fly.

God made puppies.

God made kittens.

God made elephants.

God made giraffes.

God made horses.

God made cows.

God made animals with hard shells.

God made animals with soft fur.

God made animals that crawl.

God made animals that jump.

God made fall.

God made winter.

God made spring.

God made summer.

God made everything. Thank you, God!

God Gives Me Good Things

Supplies: Fabric, scissors, glue sticks

Instructions: Before class, cut fabric into small pieces. During class, let children choose pieces of the fabric and help them glue those onto the shirt on their coloring pages. Explain how God made good things for us, like clothes to keep us warm.

God Gives Me Good Things Activities

Food Table

Supplies
- Construction paper (1 sheet per child)
- Marker
- Thin fabric
- Glue sticks
- Crayons
- O-shaped cereal

Before class, write "God Gives Me Good Things" in big letters across the top of the construction paper sheets. Cut fabric into 7" x 2" pieces to make tablecloths. Cut construction paper into one-inch circles. Give each child a paper and allow him or her to choose a tablecloth. Help children glue the tablecloth onto their papers. While some children are gluing, others can be coloring. To represent bowls, have children choose one or two circles and glue them onto the tablecloth. Children will then glue cereal rings onto the circles to represent food God gives us.

Feeling Socks

Supplies
- Adult tube sock
- Small objects that could fit inside a sock: ball, block, car, spoon, cup, apple

Put a small toy (that is easily identified by shape) inside the sock. Show children the sock and let them all have the opportunity to feel the object. What do you feel? Ask them to guess what's in the sock. When children identify the object, talk about how God gives us that thing and how we use it. For younger toddlers, you could allow them to feel it first and then pull it out and identify it by sight. Less verbal children may not say what the object is, but you can involve them by asking, "Is that a ball?" Give them the opportunity to say yes.

Beanbag Toss

Supplies
- 4 or 5 small boxes
- Magazines
- Scissors
- Glue
- 2 or 3 beanbags

Before class, cut out from the magazines several examples of good things God gives us. You could choose things such as: children's clothes, pets, food, houses, furniture, and toys. Glue one "good thing" in the bottom of each box. In class, set up the boxes in a line. Have children stand a short distance away and try to toss beanbags into the boxes. Encourage children to get the beanbag out of the box and name the picture in the box. Talk about God's good gifts.

Cleaning House

Supplies
- Small broom and dustpan
- Dustcloths
- Toy vacuum
- Paper bags
- Scrap paper
- Small table
- Toy dishes and food
- Play kitchen *(optional)*

Invite the toddlers to help clean up the room to get ready for some friends to come over. Give children various cleaning tools and show them how to use the items. Scatter some scrap paper in the area, and assign a few children to pick up the trash and put it in their paper bags. Children can also set the table with the toy dishes and food or help prepare the meal. Other children could be taking care of the babies while the rest are cooking and cleaning. Remind them that God gives us all these good things and that He is happy when we share them with our friends.

God gives me food.

Thank You, God, for food.

God gives me apples to eat.

God gives me clothes.

Thank You, God, for clothes.

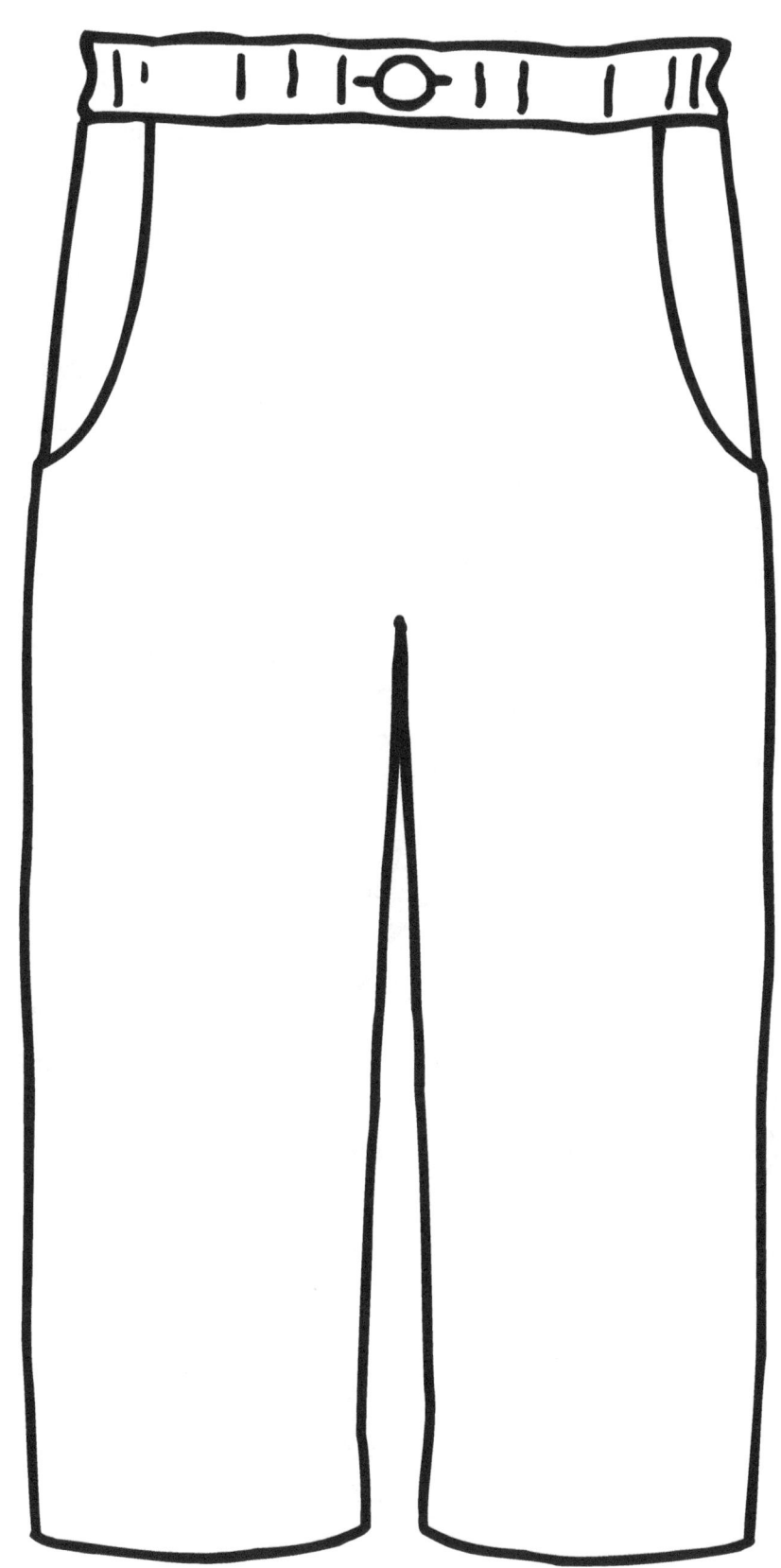

God gives me shoes.

My clothes keep me warm.

God gives me a place to live.

God gives me a place to sleep.

God gives me good things.

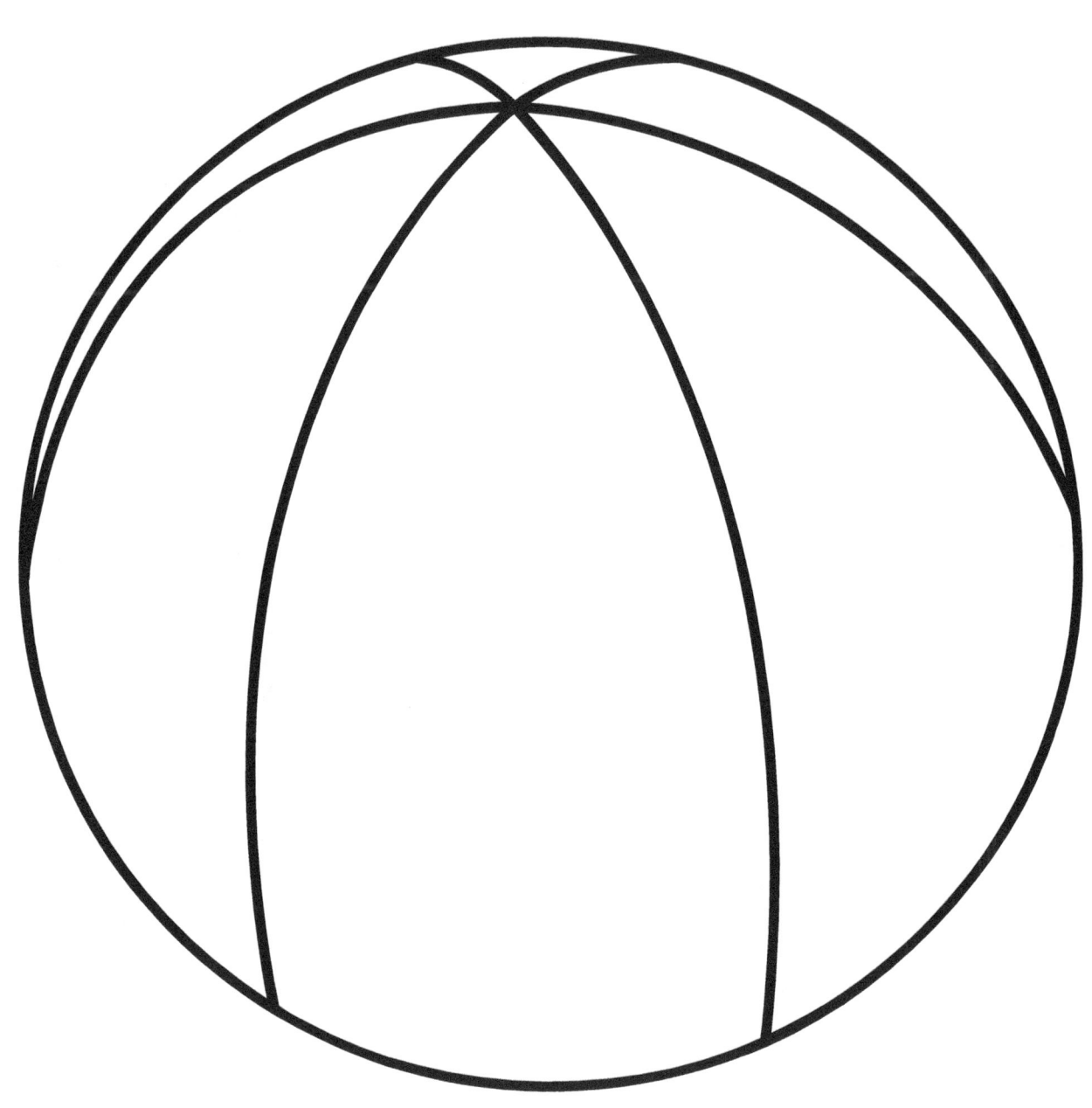

Thank You, God, for good things.

God gives me water.

Thank You, God, for good water.

God Cares for Me

Supplies: Sandpaper, scissors, glue

Instructions: Before class, cut sandpaper into small pieces so it's easier for the children to handle. During class, help the children glue their pieces of sandpaper to the sandbox on the coloring page. Remind the kids that God cares for them when they are playing.

God Cares for Me Activities

"God Cares for Me"

Sing the following song with the children to the tune of "Mary Had a Little Lamb." Lead the children in doing the motions too.

God cares for me *(point to self)*, when I sleep, *(hands folded under head)*
When I sleep, when I sleep.
God cares for me *(point to self)* when I sleep. *(hands folded under head)*
Because He loves me so. *(hands crossed on chest)*

Other Verses:
… when I wake *(yawn and stretch)*
… when I eat *(pretend to eat)*
… when I play *(pretend to toss a ball)*

Obstacle Course

Supplies
- Small table
- Small riding toy
- Toddler crawling tube *(optional)*

Set up an obstacle course for the children, using the furniture you have in your room and a few other items. For example, children could crawl under the table, ride a few feet on a riding toy, and then crawl through a toddler tube *(optional)*. For older children, you could add a small stool to climb over or chairs to run around. Tell toddlers before you start that God cares for us all day, even when we are playing. God likes for us to play because we are having fun and exercising our bodies He gave us. For younger toddlers, you can lead children through the course. While you are going through the course, keep telling the children what you are doing and what comes next.

Sleep Time

Supplies
- Large blanket
- Small blankets or pillows
- Flashlight
- Pop-up tent *(optional)*

Before class, set up a pop-up tent or drape a blanket over some chairs to create a tent. Slightly dim the lights. Give each child a small pillow or blanket and tell the children they are going to have a sleep time. Remind them that God cares for them and is watching over them, even when they are sleeping. Guide the children to the tent with your flashlight. Help everyone to get into the tent and to lie down with their pillows. Pray a good-night prayer together, remembering to thank God that He cares for us all the time. You could also sing a quiet version of "Jesus Loves Me" or another favorite, before ending the sleep time.

Sunshine Sun Catcher

Supplies
- Yellow tissue paper
- Pen
- Scissors
- Clear adhesive covering
- Glue stick

Before class, trace and cut 4" circles from yellow tissue paper. Also cut out large triangular sunrays of various sizes. Cut clear adhesive covering into 10" lengths. Then remove the backing and fold the covering in half length-wise, smoothing out the bubbles as much as possible. Cut the clear covering into 7" circles. Give each child a clear circle and a tissue paper circle. Help children glue the yellow circle to the middle of the clear circle. Children can then pick out some sun rays to glue around the edge of the yellow circle. Remind children that God cares for them when they wake up and all day long.

God cares for me in the morning.

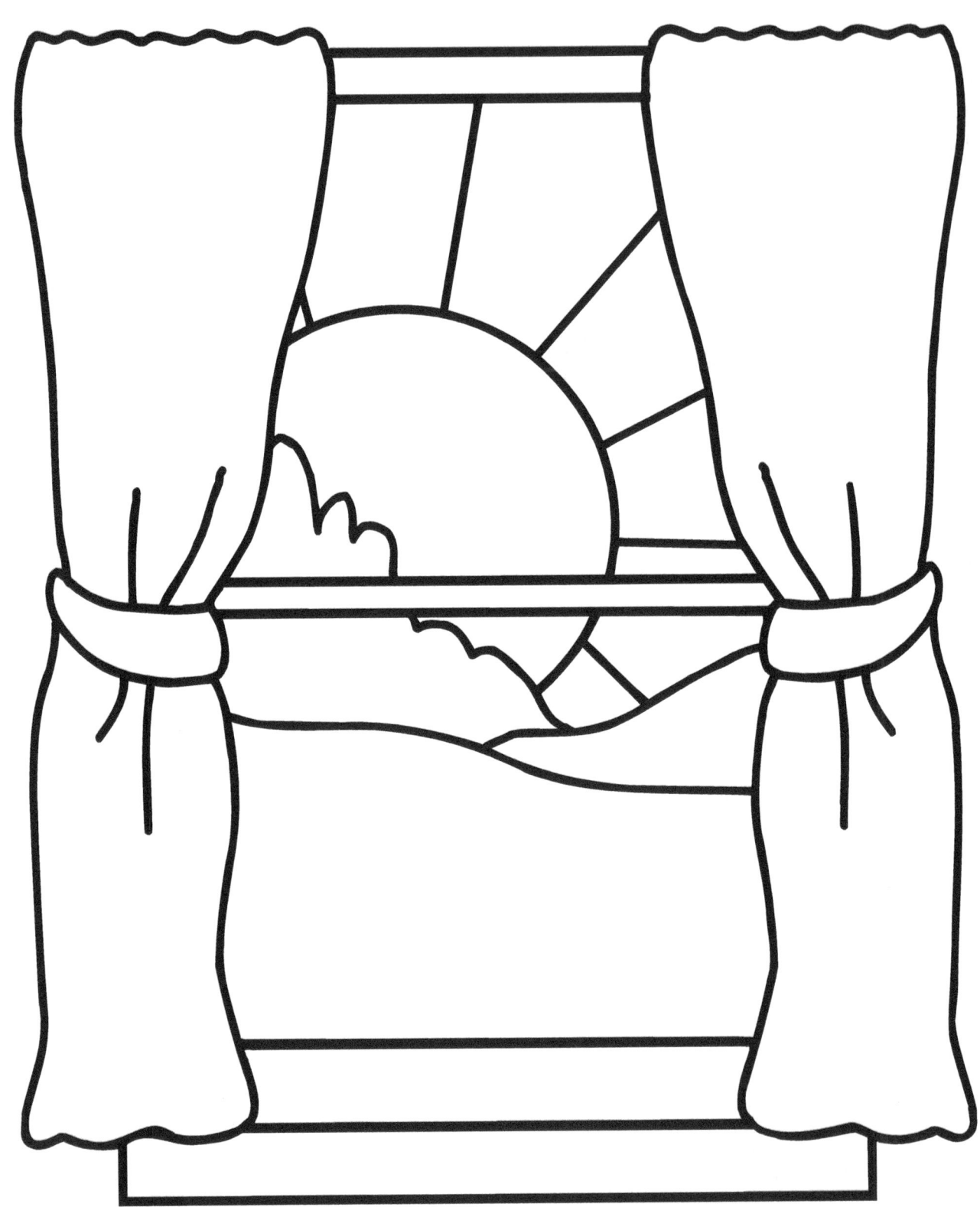

God cares for me when I am waking up.

God cares for me when I am eating.

God cares for me when I am thirsty.

God cares for me when I am playing.

God cares for me when I am playing.

God cares for me when I go to new places.

God cares for me at night.

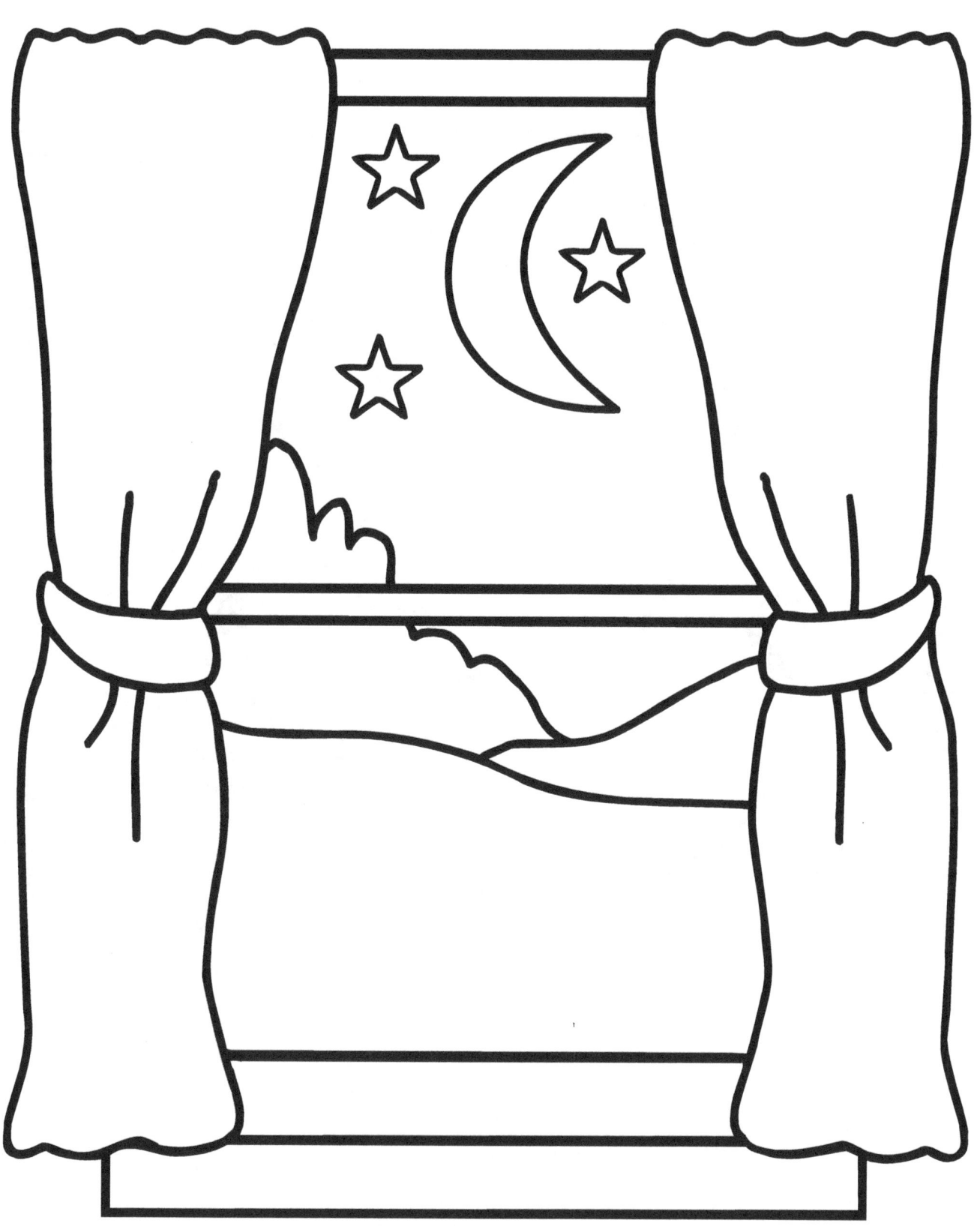

God cares for me when I am sleeping.

Jesus Loves Me

Supplies: Foil, scissors, glue sticks

Instructions: Before class, cut foil into squares, rectangles, and ovals. During class, help children glue foil, shiny side up, onto the mirror frames. Help the kids press down on their foil pieces, look into them, and say, "Jesus loves me."

Jesus Loves Me Activities

Fingerprint Pictures

Supplies
- White paper
- Pen
- Washable ink pads
- Large crayons
- Moist towelettes

Before class, write "Jesus Loves _____" along the top of a piece of paper, one per child. Draw a circle on each paper for the children to decorate as a face. As children get their papers, write each child's name in the blank. Talk about how Jesus loves them and how each one of them is very special. Even their fingerprints are different! Help children place their fingers on the washable ink pads and use their fingerprints to decorate the face on their paper. Help children make features and any other type of decoration. Children can also use crayons to color their faces. When children are finished using the ink pads, wash the ink off their hands in a sink or with moist towelettes.

The Jesus Loves Me Jump

Supplies
- Construction paper
- White paper
- Picture of Jesus
- Markers
- Tape
- Marker
- Masking tape
- Magazine *(optional)*

Before class, write "Jesus" in large letters on a sheet of construction paper. Tape a picture of Jesus on the paper. Write "Loves" on a sheet of white paper and also draw a red heart. On another sheet of white paper, write "Me" and draw a picture of a child (or use one from a magazine). Tape these three pieces of paper to the floor, about 2' apart. Line up the children, and ask them to jump over each piece of paper, one at a time. Older or more verbal children can say the word on the paper as they jump over it. For younger toddlers, the teacher can say the word while the toddler jumps or walks over it. After a child completes three jumps, he or she can run back to the line and tag the next child. Continue until all children have had an opportunity to jump.

"Jesus Loves Me"

Sing the following to the tune of "Old McDonald Had a Farm." Lead children in doing the motions too, and encourage them to sing along.

Jesus loves me; yes, He does *(point to self)*
And He loves you too. *(point to others)*
Jesus loves me; yes, He does *(point to self)*
And He loves you too! *(point to others)*
(At this part, leader sings the names of individual children and points to them. Make sure to sing it enough times that all children are included.)
He loves Tanya, He loves Sam, He loves Jamal, and He loves Anisha! *(point to children as you name them)*

(All sing ending)
Jesus loves me; yes, He does *(point to self)*
And He loves you too! *(point to others)*

See Who Jesus Loves

Supplies
- Paper towel or toilet paper tubes, 1 for each child
- Stickers (Jesus stickers, if possible)
- Pictures of people *(optional)*

Give each child a tube and some stickers. Help children apply the stickers on their tubes. You should have a tube too. Look through your tube and say, "Let's see who Jesus loves. Oh, I see Maria. Jesus loves Maria!" Have children look around the room for someone Jesus loves. Encourage children to look at one another through their tubes. If you have posters displayed on the wall, ask children to look at the posters to see more people Jesus loves. You can also sit in a circle and ask children to take turns looking through the tube and finding someone Jesus loves. Help younger and less verbal children by naming the child they are looking at.

Jesus loves everyone.

Jesus loves mothers.

Jesus loves fathers.

Jesus loves families.

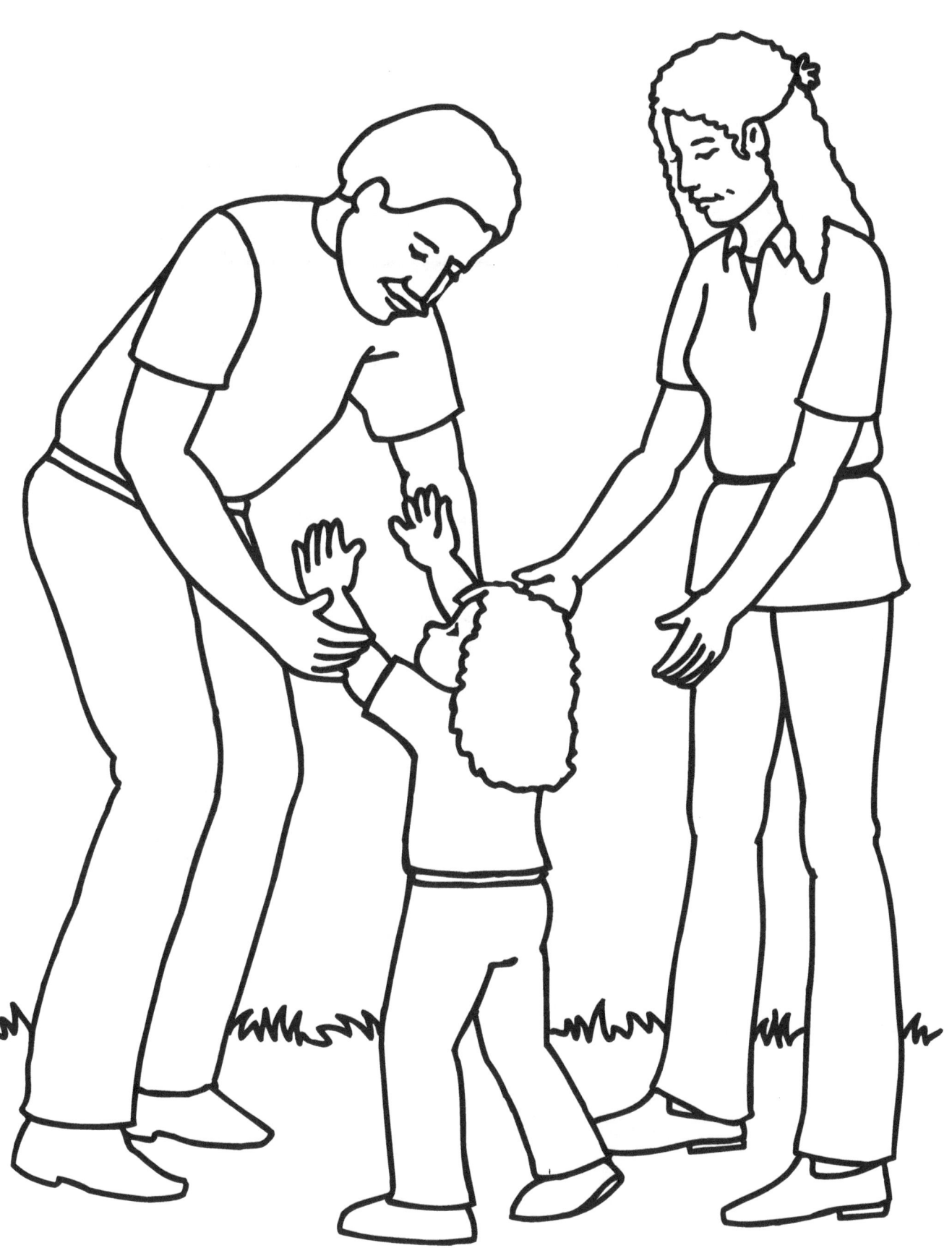

Jesus loves families.

I love my family.

Jesus loves children.

Jesus loves children.

Jesus loves children.

Jesus loves children.

Jesus loves you too!

Jesus loves people.

Jesus loves people.

Jesus loves people.

Jesus loves people.

Jesus loves people.

Jesus loves you.

Jesus loves me.

I Go to Church

Supplies: Tissue paper (various colors), glue sticks

Instructions: Before class, tear tissue paper into various small sizes and shapes. During class, let each child choose pieces of paper to glue onto the stained-glass windows of the church building. Allow the children to show the class the colors they chose for their windows. Remind children that we go to church to learn more about God.

I Go to Church Activities

Going to Church

Supplies
- Stuffed animal or baby doll, 1 for each child
- Children's Bible
- Blanket
- Crackers
- Paper plates

Spread a blanket in the corner of the room with a children's Bible, crackers, and paper plates nearby. Give each child a stuffed animal or doll. Tell children to follow you and take their animals to church. When you get to the blanket, encourage children to sit down and have their animals or dolls sit down too. Start by singing a simple worship song together. Then read a story from the children's Bible, holding the book up so children and their animals can see. Have prayer time, encouraging children to fold their hands. Then give each child crackers for snack time.

Praise God Shakers

Supplies
- Paper lunch bags
- Large crayons
- Stickers of crosses, Bibles, Jesus, churches
- Oyster crackers
- Bowl
- Large spoons
- Tape
- Electronic device *(optional)*

Give each child a paper bag. Encourage children to make colorful designs on both sides of their bags. Write each child's name near the bottom of his or her bag. After children color, give them stickers to decorate their bags. Put a scoop of oyster crackers in each bag. Older children can hold the bag while you put the crackers inside. Fold down the bag a few times and tape it shut. Tell children that they're going to sing because we want to praise God. Sing "Jesus Loves the Little Children" or a similar song and encourage children to sing and shake their bags. You could also play children's worship songs and have them sing along with their new shakers.

Finding Bibles

Supplies
- Small Bibles, 1 for each child
- Construction paper
- Scissors
- Stickers of Jesus
- Tape

Before class, attach stickers of Jesus to small pieces of construction paper, and tape them inside the front covers of small Bibles. Scatter the Bibles around the room. Help each child find a Bible and hold it. Then ask children to sit down with you in a circle. Tell them to open their Bibles and find a picture of Jesus. Remind children that Jesus loves them very much. You might also want to read them a story from an illustrated Bible.

Sponge Ball

Supplies
- Plastic grocery bag
- New, hand-size sponges

Before class, put the sponges into the grocery bag. During class, dump the sponges onto the floor. Ask children to help you stuff them into the bag as you hold it. Tie a secure knot on the bag, tightening it so the sponges form a ball inside the bag. Remind children of the things they do at church: sing, pray, learn about Jesus, and play with their friends. Have children stand in a circle and throw the sponge ball to one another. You can also show children how to kick the ball back and forth. Be sure that everyone gets a turn. For young toddlers, you can sit in a circle and pass the ball while singing a song.

I learn about Jesus at church.
I am happy at church.

I sing at church.

I sing about Jesus.

I can pray at church.
I am happy at church.

I pray at church.

God hears me pray.

I learn at church.

I learn from my teacher.

I learn God loves me.

I learn about Jesus.

I have friends at church.

I am a friend to others.

God gives me friends.

God Makes a Promise

Supplies: Glue sticks, large crayons

Instructions: Tell the children to color their rainbows pretty colors. Explain that the rainbow was a sign of God's promise to Noah. Once they are done coloring, let each child choose jumbo cotton balls and help them glue the cotton onto the cloud shapes. Remind children that God keeps His promises.

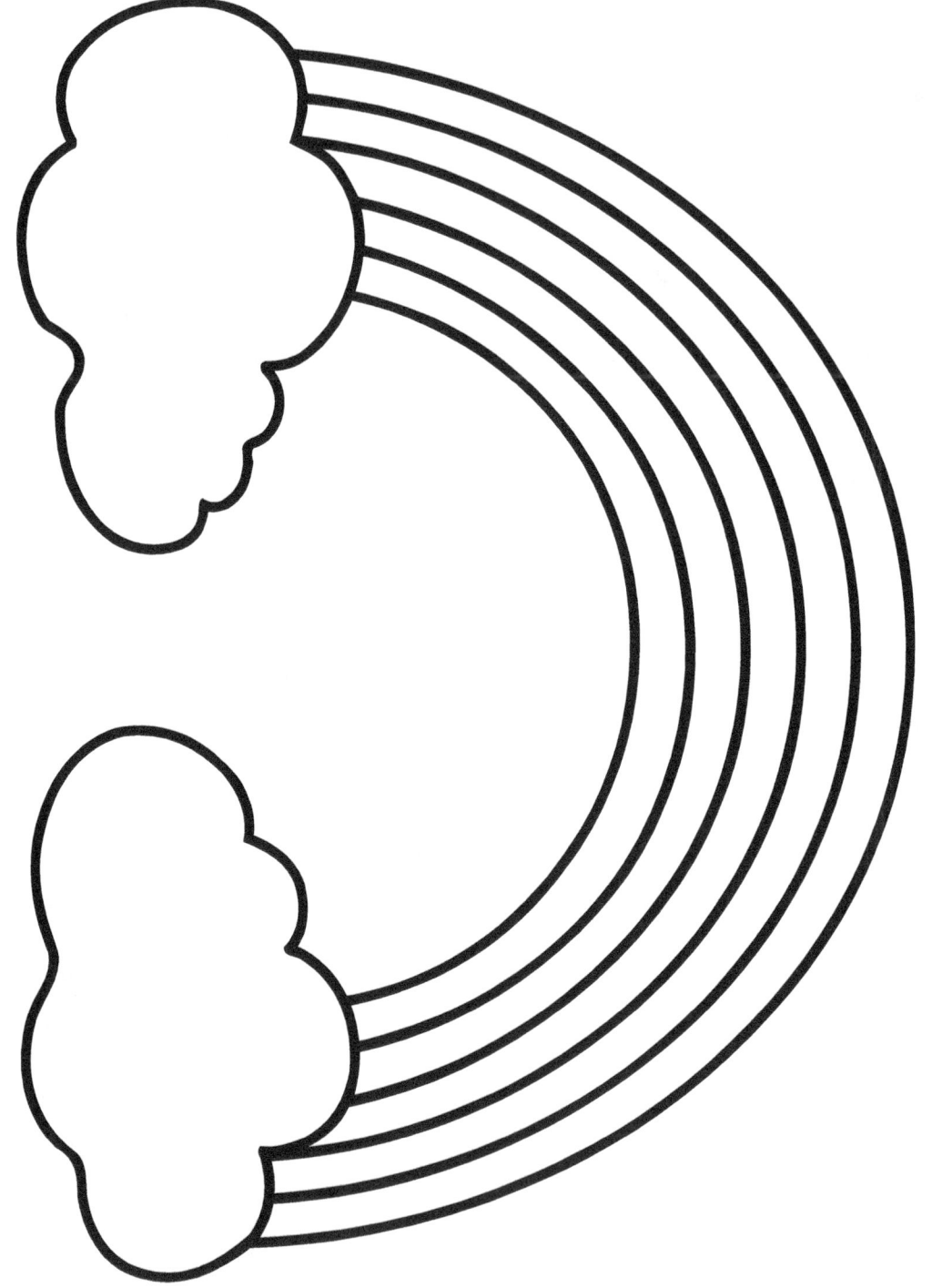

Noah Activities

Rainbow in a Bag

Supplies
- Water
- 3 boxes of colorful fruit gelatin: blue, red, and yellow
- Small pan
- Wooden spoon
- Stove
- 3 small bowls
- Heavy, resealable plastic freezer bags
- Masking tape

Before class, prepare each gelatin separately. Chill in the refrigerator for 20 minutes, until partially set and thickened. Stir a few times during the 20 minutes. Take the bowls out of the refrigerator and leave out until class, but not for too long. Spoon the three colors of gelatin into several heavy, resealable plastic freezer bags. The bags should not be too full. Zip the bags closed, double-bag them, and seal with masking tape to prevent leaks. In class, give children the bags to squeeze and knead. Show children how the colors blend together to make rainbows. Explain how this reminds us of the rainbow God put in the sky when He promised Noah that He would never again flood the earth.

Rainmaker

Supplies
- Foam cups, 1 for each child
- Sharpened pencil
- Crayons
- Large plastic tub
- Water
- Towels

Before class, turn over the foam cups and use a pencil to gently make small holes in the bottoms of the cups. Fill a large tub with water, and place towels under it. In class, give each child a cup. Let children color their cups. Then take children to the tub of water and show them how they can watch it rain. Show children how to fill their cups and hold them over the tub, watching as it rains! Remind children that, for Noah, it rained for 40 days and nights.

Animal Sounds

Supplies
- Box
- Toy animals

In class, gather the children around the box full of toy animals. Tell children that these are some of the same animals Noah took with him on the big boat. When you hold up an animal, ask children to tell you the sound that animal makes. Help children if they don't know what sound it makes. Next, have each child pick an animal from the box and the class can imitate the sound that animal makes. The children could also show how that animal walks. For example, the children could pretend to fly like birds!

Building the Boat

Supplies
- Brown paper grocery bags, at least 10
- Newspaper
- Masking tape
- Toy hammers, saws, and other tools
- Wooden blocks
- Fine sandpaper

Before class, stuff at least ten grocery bags with crumpled newspaper, about half full. Fold over the tops of the bags and secure with masking tape. These are the pieces of "wood" children can use to build a boat. In class, give each child a tool and tell him or her to help you build the boat. Guide them to line up the bags and make an outline of a boat. Allow them to hammer and saw the "wood." You can also give them blocks on which they can hammer and saw. Other children can use the sandpaper to sand the blocks. Talk about how Noah obeyed God and spent a lot of time building the big boat.

Noah was a good man.

God told Noah to build a big boat.

Noah worked hard.

Noah obeyed God.

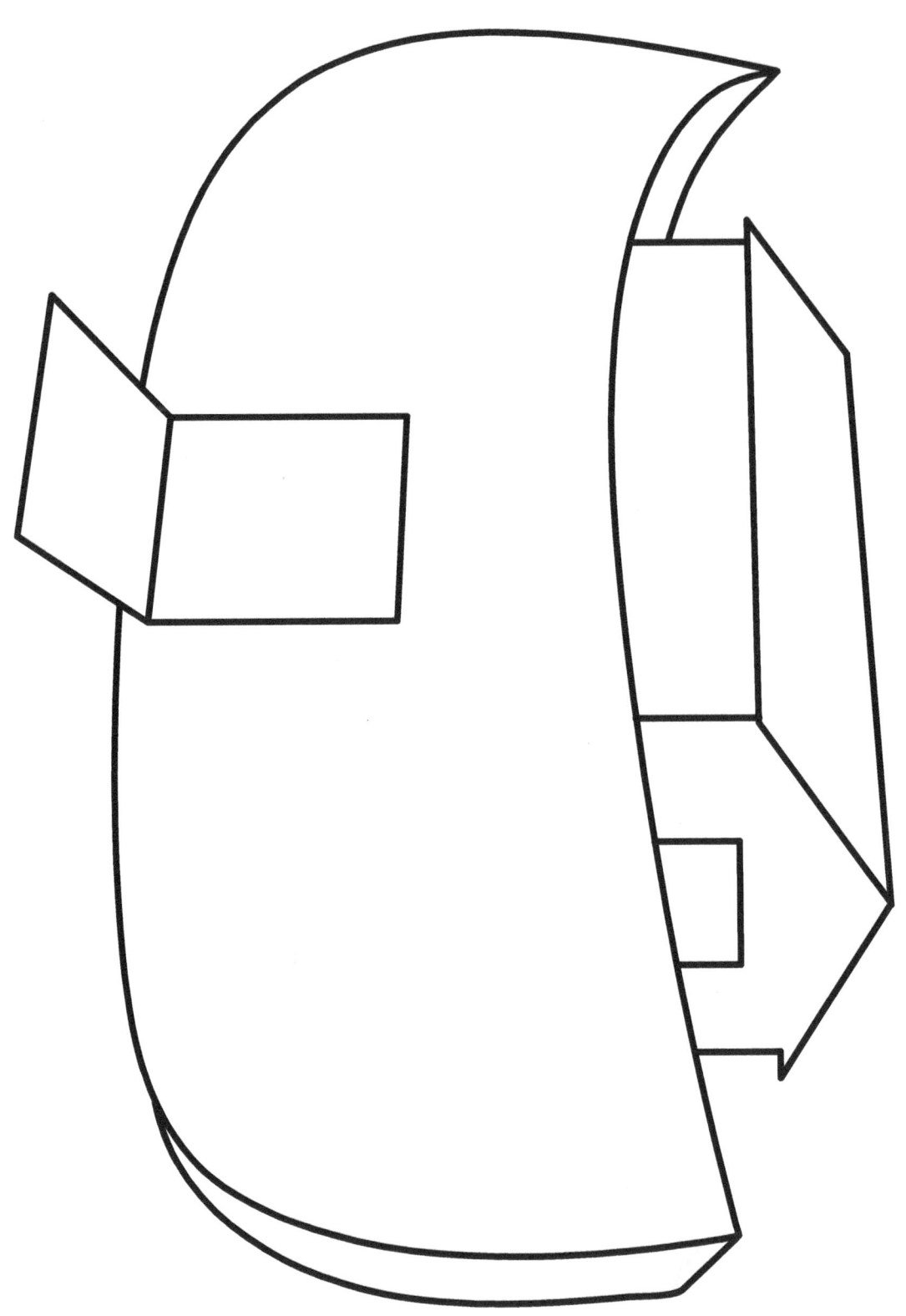

Noah loved God and built a big boat.

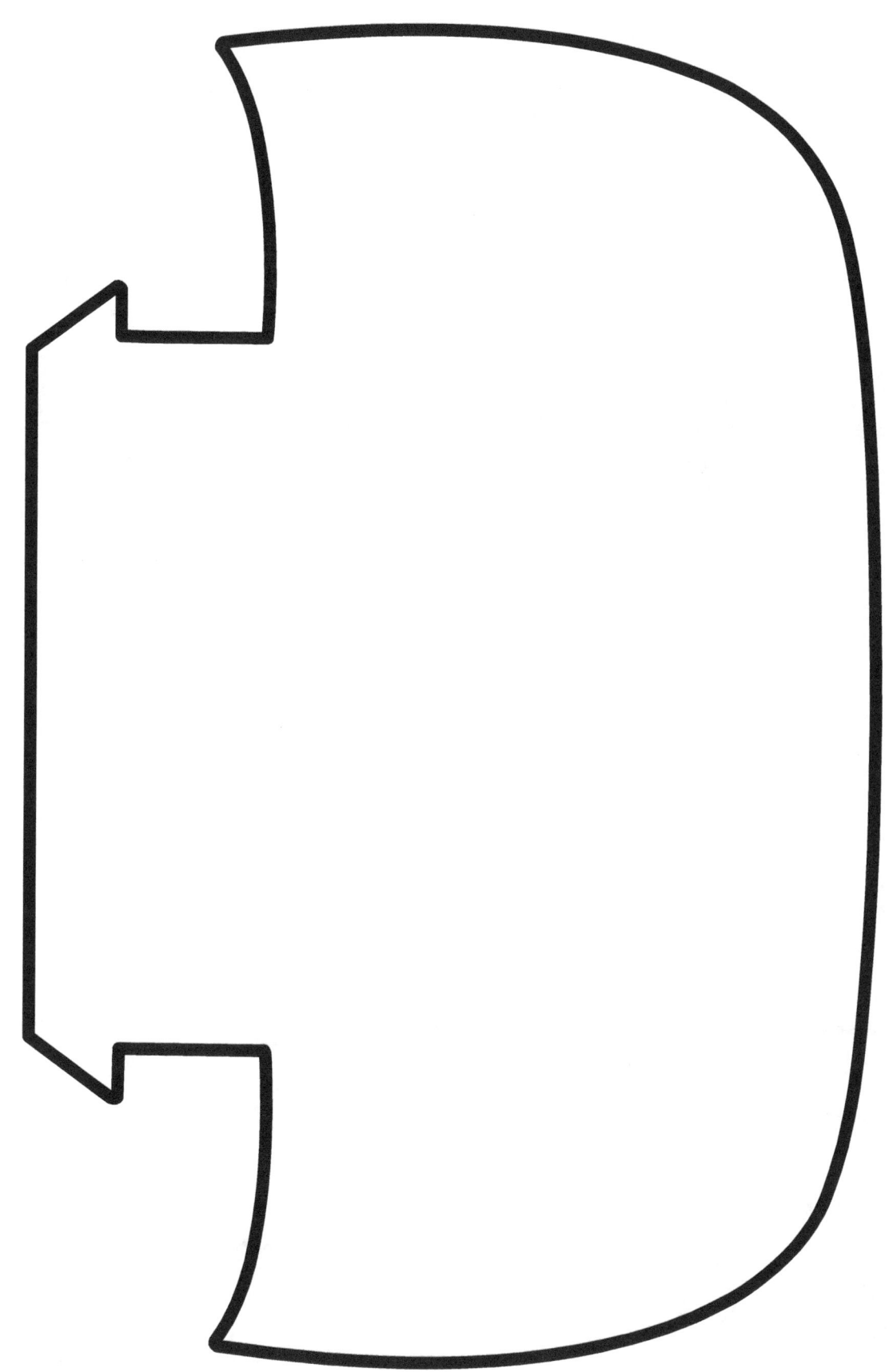

Noah brought animals into the ark.

Noah brought two of every animal.

Noah brought tall animals.

Noah brought big animals.

Noah brought small animals.

The animals got into the boat.

God sent rain.

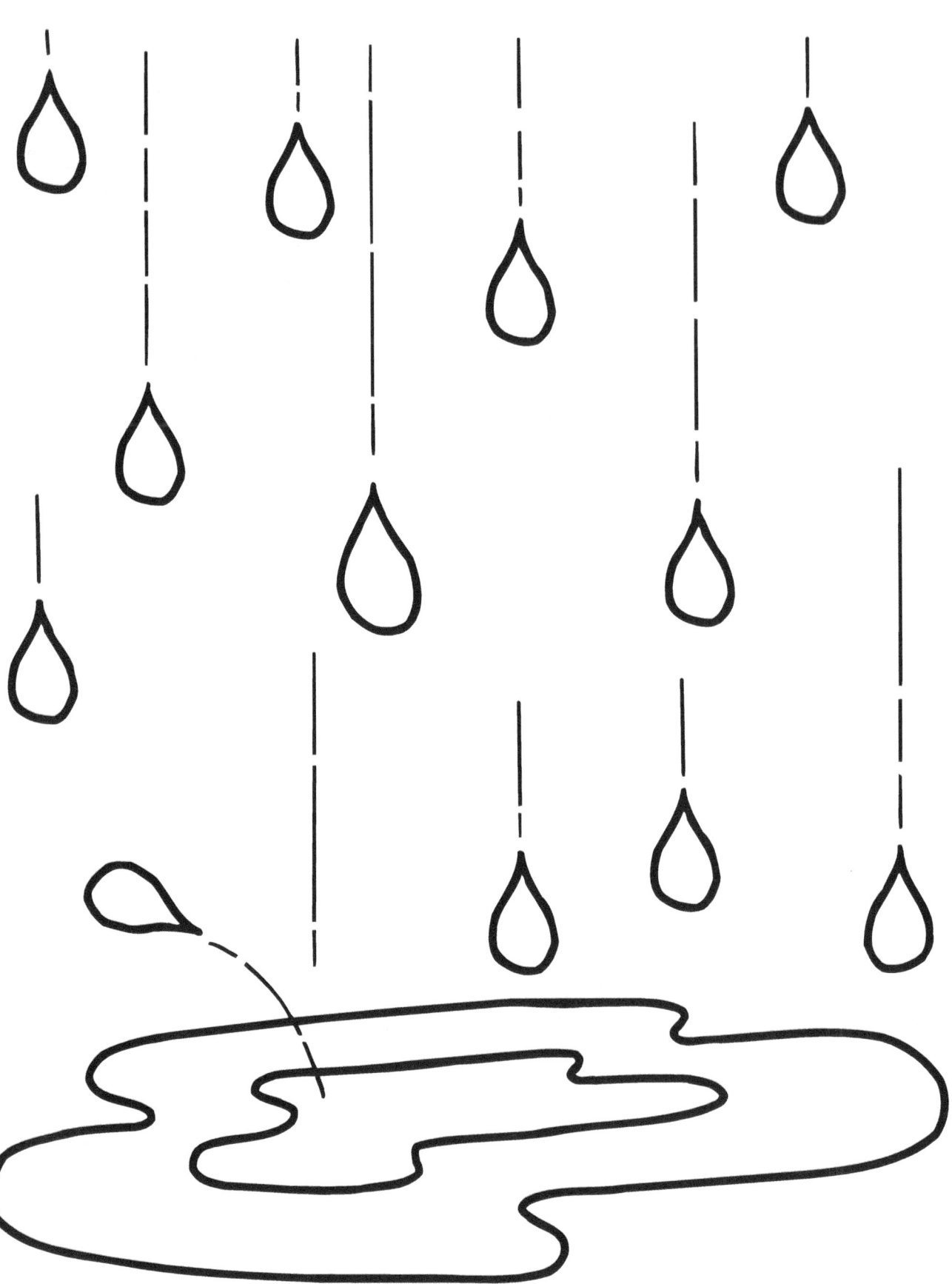

There was a flood.

The ark floated on the water.

The rain stopped.

God put a rainbow in the sky.

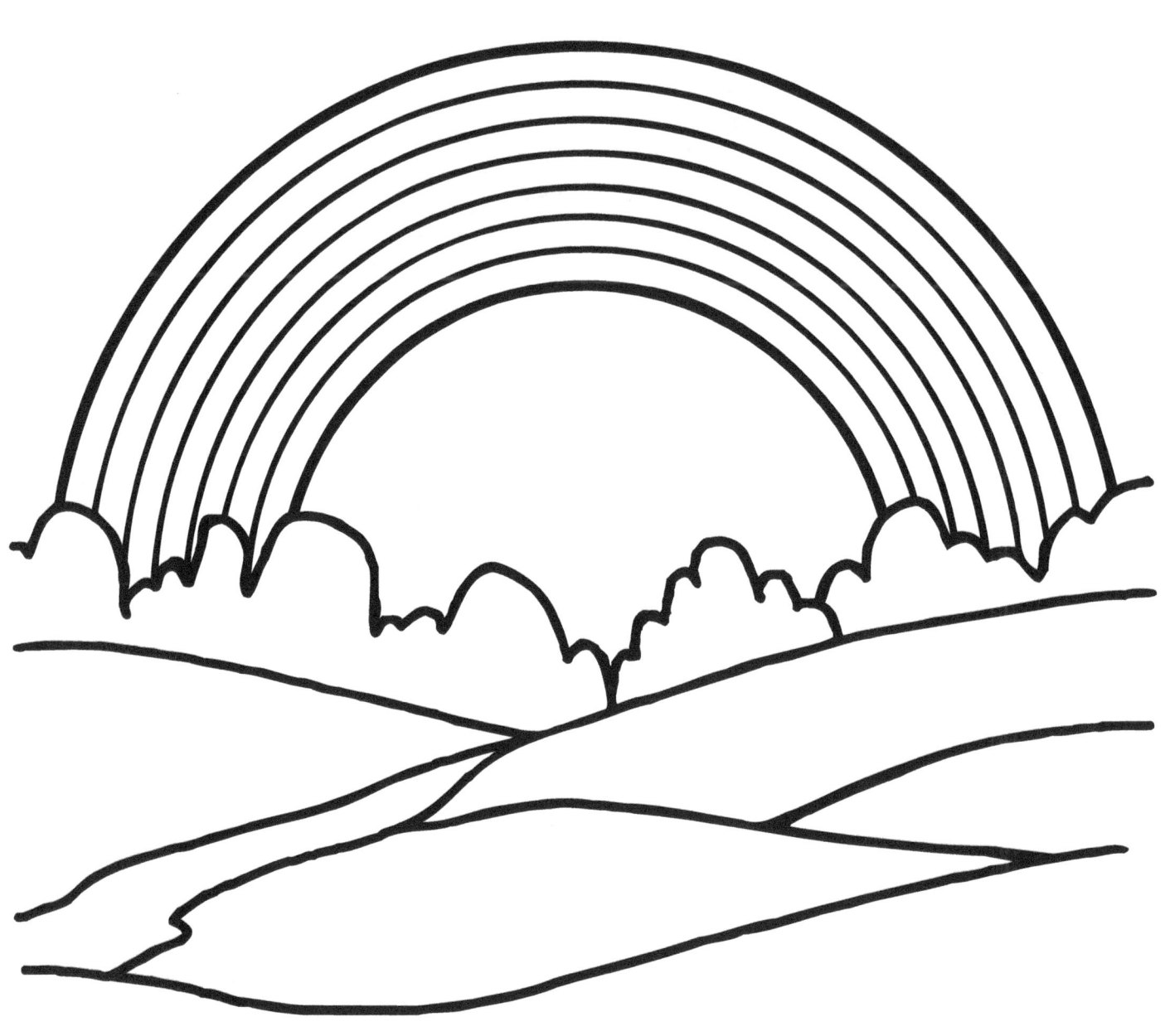

Baby Jesus Was Born

Supplies: Strips of hay, yellow paper, or wide raffia; glue sticks

Instructions: Have children choose some materials to use as the hay in baby Jesus' manger. Once they have their hay, help chidren glue it onto their manger. Remind children that Jesus was a baby just like they once were.

Baby Jesus Activities

Following the Star

Supplies
- Yellow or white card stock or construction paper
- Scissors
- Glitter
- Glue
- Flashlights
- Child-safe nativity set
- Yarn

Before class, cut star shapes out of card stock or paper and decorate with glitter. Make one larger star to represent the star that led the wise men to Jesus. Attach stars to yarn and suspend from the ceiling. Display the large star in a corner of the room, above the nativity set. In class, gather the children and give each one a flashlight. Tell children that they are going to follow the star and find baby Jesus. Tell children to aim their flashlights at the stars, which will sparkle when the light hits them. Dim the lights and lead the children in walking around the room. Talk about how the wise men followed the star to find baby Jesus. Tell the children to find the large star and follow it to the nativity set. Show the children baby Jesus in the manger. Sing "Away in a Manger."

Peek-a-Boo Boxes

Supplies
- Small boxes with lids, shoe-box size or smaller
- Christmas wrapping paper
- Scissors
- Tape
- Bows
- Small items from a nativity set: baby Jesus, Mary figure, Joseph figure, donkey, manger, hay, angel, star

Before class, wrap the boxes and lids with Christmas paper. Put bows on top of the lids. Inside each box, place an item that relates to the story of Jesus' birth. In class, tell children they are going to look inside the Peek-a-Boo Boxes. Have a child open a box and peek inside. Ask the child to tell what he or she sees. If the child sees hay, for example, talk about how Jesus was born in a place where animals lived and hay was probably all around. Continue until each child has had the opportunity to peek inside a box and talk about what they see.

Pencil Holder Gifts

Supplies
- Clean, plastic frozen juice containers, 1 for each child
- Construction paper
- Tape or glue sticks
- Stickers
- Marker

Before class, cover the juice containers with paper so that the labels are covered. Say to the children, "You are going to make gifts to give someone to celebrate Jesus' birth. Jesus is God's gift to us, and it's fun to give gifts to others!" Give each child an empty container. Help children to choose stickers to decorate the containers. Once children have finished decorating, write on the pencil holder: "This is a gift from: _____"

Christmas Card Puzzles

Supplies
- Christmas cards with pictures relating to Jesus' birth
- Clear adhesive covering
- Scissors

Before class, gather Christmas cards that have pictures of baby Jesus, Mary and Joseph, the stable, manger, angels, shepherds, and the wise men. Cut off the front of the cards and cover with clear adhesive covering. Cut each card in half, curving each cut to look like a puzzle piece. With the children, scatter the card pieces around on the floor or table. (You should only use two or three puzzles at the same time.) Ask the children to help you match the halves together. As the children fit together the cards, ask them about the pictures they've made. Talk about that part of the Christmas story and then continue with another card. For older children, you can cut each card into four pieces to make it more challenging.

Birthday Party for Jesus

Supplies
- Red and green streamers
- Colorful balloons
- Party hats
- Tape
- Colored paper, folded in half
- Large crayons
- Nativity and star stickers
- Electronic device
- Noisemakers
- Cupcakes

Before class, decorate the room for a birthday party. Display streamers and balloons (out of reach of children), and make a "Happy Birthday Jesus" sign to display. Tell children that they are having a birthday party for Jesus! Give each child a party hat. Help children make cards by coloring the folded paper and putting on stickers. You can play a game like Musical Bumps, in which you play songs about Jesus' birth, while children jump or dance. When the music stops, everyone sits down as fast as they can. At snack time, pray and thank God for sending Jesus to earth. Give each child a noisemaker and sing a happy birthday song to Jesus. Then give each child a cupcake. Throughout the party, remind children that Christmas is Jesus' birthday.

Joseph and Mary were married.

Mary was Jesus' mother.

Jesus was born.

Baby Jesus was born.

Jesus is God's Son.

Joseph and Mary loved Jesus.

Angels sang the night Jesus was born.

Shepherds came to visit Jesus.

The shepherds visited Jesus.

The shepherds were happy Jesus was born.

Wise men saw a star.

The star led the wise men to Jesus.

The wise men gave Jesus gifts.

Toddlers & 2s Scope and Sequence

Fall
God Made My Eyes	10–11
God Made My Ears	12–13
God Made My Nose	14–16
God Made My Mouth	17–18
God Made My Arms	19–20
God Made My Hands	21–22
God Made My Legs	23–25
God Made My Feet	26–28
God Made All of Me	29–31
God Gives Vegetables	55–57
God Gives Fruit	58–59, 111
God Gives Cereal and Bread	60–61
God Gives Water and Juice	62–63, 120–122

Winter
Joseph and Mary Loved Jesus	200
Baby Jesus Was Born	195–201
Shepherds Visited Jesus	202–204
Wise Men Worshipped Jesus	205–207
God Gives Me Food	109–111
God Gives Me Clothes	112–115
God Gives Me a Home	116–117
God Gives Me Water	120–122
God Gives Me Good Things	118–119
God Made Babies	35–37
God Made Bigger Children	38–40
God Made Families	41–46
God Made People to Help Us	47–51

Spring
I Sing at Church	160–161
I Pray at Church	162–164
I Learn about Jesus at Church	159, 165–168
I Have Friends at Church	169–171
Jesus Loves Families	139–143
Jesus Loves Children	144–147
Jesus Loves All People	138, 149–153
Jesus Loves Me	148, 154–155
God Made the Sky	67–68
God Made Water and Land	69, 78–81
God Made Trees and Plants	85–88
God Made the Sun, Moon, and Stars	75–77
God Made Everything	101–105

Summer
God Made Birds	70–74
God Made Fish	82–84
God Made Little Animals	89–92
God Made Big Animals	93–96
God Made All the Animals	97–100
Noah Builds a Boat	175–179
Animals Enter the Boat	180–185
Rain Comes Down	186–189
The Rainbow	190
God Cares for Me When I'm Waking Up	126–127
God Cares for Me When I'm Eating	128–129
God Cares for Me When I'm Playing	130–132
God Cares for Me When I'm Sleeping	133–134